Strategies for the Threshold #6

Dealing with Resheph:
Spirit of Trouble

Anne Hamilton

Irenie Senior

Dealing with Resheph: Spirit of Trouble

Strategies for the Threshold #6

© Anne Hamilton 2020

Published by Armour Books

P. O. Box 492, Corinda QLD 4075

Cover Images: © iloveotto | Canstockphoto;
© Kevin Carden | Little girl in fierce battle;
© Laura College | Unsplash

Deer icons by Carrie Stephens, Bakara and Viktoria.1703
Maps by Beckon Creative

Interior Design and Typeset by Beckon Creative

ISBN: 978-1-925380-316

A catalogue record for this book is available from the National Library of Australia

All rights reserved. No part of this publication may be reproduced, stored in, or introduced into a retrieval system, or transmitted, in any form, or by any means (electronic, mechanical, photocopying, recording or otherwise) without the prior written permission of the publisher.

Note: Australian spelling and grammar conventions are used throughout this book.

Strategies for the Threshold #6

Dealing with Resheph:
Spirit of Trouble

Anne Hamilton
Irenie Senior

Scripture quotations marked BLB are taken from The Blue Letter Bible. Used by permission. blueletterbible.org

Scripture quotations marked BSB are taken from The Holy Bible, Berean Study Bible, BSB Copyright ©2016 by Bible Hub Used by Permission. All Rights Reserved Worldwide.

Scripture quotations marked ESV are taken from the ESV® Bible (The Holy Bible, English Standard Version®), copyright © 2001 by Crossway, a publishing ministry of Good News Publishers. Used by permission. All rights reserved.

Scripture quotations marked GNT are from the Good News Translation in Today's English Version—Second Edition Copyright © 1992 by American Bible Society. Used by Permission.

Scripture quotations marked KJV are taken from the King James Version of the Bible. Public domain.

Scripture quotations marked NASB are taken from the New American Standard Bible®, Copyright © 1960, 1962, 1963, 1968, 1971, 1972, 1973, 1975, 1977, 1995 by The Lockman Foundation. Used by permission. (www.Lockman.org)

Scripture quotations marked NLT are taken from the Holy Bible, New Living Translation, copyright 1996, 2004. Used by permission of Tyndale House Publishers, Inc., Wheaton, Illinois 60189. All rights reserved.

Scripture quotations marked NIV are taken from the Holy Bible, New International Version®, NIV®. Copyright © 1973, 1978, 1984, 2011 by Biblica, Inc.™ Used by permission of Zondervan. All rights reserved worldwide. www.zondervan.com The "NIV" and "New International Version" are trademarks registered in the United States Patent and Trademark Office by Biblica, Inc.™.

Scripture quotations marked NKJV are taken from the New King James Version. Copyright © 1982 by Thomas Nelson, Inc. Used by permission. All rights reserved.

Scripture quotations marked TPT are taken from The Passion Translation®, Isaiah: The Vision copyright © 2018 by Passion & Fire Ministries, Inc. Used by permission. All rights reserved. ThePassionTranslation.com

Other Books By

Anne Hamilton

In this series

Dealing with Python: Spirit of Constriction
(with *Arpana Dev Sangamithra*)
Dealing with Ziz: Spirit of Forgetting
Name Covenant: Invitation to Friendship
Hidden in the Cleft: True and False Refuge
Dealing with Leviathan: Spirit of Retaliation

Devotional Theology series

God's Poetry: The Identity & Destiny Encoded in Your Name
God's Panoply: The Armour of God & the Kiss of Heaven
God's Pageantry: The Threshold Guardians & the Covenant Defender
God's Pottery: The Sea of Names & the Pierced Inheritance
God's Priority: World-Mending & Generational Testing
More Precious than Pearls (with *Natalie Tensen*)
As Resplendent As Rubies (with *Natalie Tensen*)
Spiritual Legal Rights (with *Janice Sergison*)

Jesus and the Healing of History Series

Like Wildflowers, Suddenly
Bent World, Bright Wings
Silk Shadows, Rings of Gold
The Singing Silence

Thank you

Beck

Cathie

David

Geraldine

Irenie

Janine

'Jim'

Jim

Natalie

and especially my mum

who once again wrote

the prayers at the end

of each chapter

Contents

Introduction		11
1	**Ancient Loyalties**	15
2	**Weeping for the Children**	55
3	**A Long Awakening**	83
4	**Paths of the Dead**	111
5	**The Harrowing**	139
6	**The Author and Finisher**	165
7	**The Deer at the Dawn of the Day**	205
Appendix 1	Summary	221
Appendix 2	Comparison of Resheph and Leviathan	224
Appendix 3	Some Persian Words	226
Appendix 4	On the Jealousy of God	228
Endnotes		229

Introduction

'EYES RIGHT!'

In the once-popular children's novel, *Grinny*, an alien invader is subjected to the juvenile game, *Eyes Right*. It's a practical joke that basically amounts to a fixed stare, slightly beyond the right shoulder of the person you're talking to. It's annoying and frustrating and, apart from putting fictional aliens at a serious disadvantage, not much practical use at all.

But what if the game went on for years? And what if we were on the receiving end? What if angelic powers were playing it on us, hypnotically pulling our attention to one side so we'd miss the obvious?

I've come to feel a bit like that as I've researched Resheph. As if there's been a spiritual game going on, and our eyes have been directed to the wrong spot for so many centuries we've now got permanent astigmatism. *Eyes right* has become our normal. That would be fine if our eyes were fixed on Jesus, but all too often that's not the case.

Whenever I'm looking at the tactics and agenda of any particular threshold spirit, the most important questions I have are: *Jesus, how did You overcome this spirit? Where? When? What did You say? What are the specific circumstances so that I, as Your disciple, can follow You?*

With Python, the answers are obvious: the temptation in the wilderness, the healing of the man at the Pool of Bethesda, the denial of Peter in the courtyard of Caiaphas and his subsequent restoration. Clear marks of Python are all over these specific events.

With Ziz, they're also obvious: the appointment of Mary Magdalene as a guardian of memory; the events on the cross including the eclipse and the giving of hyssop to Jesus. Clear marks of Ziz are all over these specific events too.

But with Leviathan, it's not at all obvious. The details—the tiny confirming clues—are missing. They simply should not be.

When Jesus took on Asherah, the so-called 'Mistress of Serpents' who also claimed the title, 'She Who Walks on Water', there's no doubt about the identity of His adversary. Nor—when He went up against her consort, Tammuz, the one whose worshippers referred to him as the 'Bread come down from Heaven'—was there anything subtle about His actions either. The same is true for the goat-human hybrid demi-god, Pan, as well as for over seventy other godlings, goddesses and deified heroes.[1]

But for Leviathan—the one who gets an entire chapter in the book of Job, and whom many commentators finger as the arch-villain in the Garden of Eden—the indicators are indistinct, ambiguous and even dubious. The signs of conflict should not be so imprecise—not when other combat zones are so clearly laid out. Yet, if Leviathan was indeed also known as Resheph, it's a different story. The markers are so obvious, it's merely a walk in the park to find them. Or rather, to be more accurate, a walk in the garden.

So my aim in this book is to remove some astigmatism that might be causing defects in our vision of the spiritual world. It's to introduce a spiritual potentate which, if I have read all the details correctly, is Leviathan by another name. Most importantly of all, it's to show the unparalleled artistry of Jesus in completing the work of an ancient repair and so, once again, healing history.

Of course, as usual, this book is designed with sections that use 'numerical literary style', the beautiful fusion of words and numbers that characterise the epistles and gospels. And, of course, again as usual, it's not the last word on the subject, just the opening of a dialogue on a topic that seems to be long forgotten.

In preparing this volume I have repeatedly prayed nothing here constitutes an invitation for Leviathan-Resheph to manifest in any way as you read on. Paul wrote, *'We should not be outwitted by Satan; for we are not ignorant of his schemes.'* (2 Corinthians 2:11 BLB) That might have been true two millennia ago, but it certainly isn't the case any longer. We don't even know of the existence of Resheph, let alone what Jesus achieved regarding it.

This book aims to begin the rectification of our ignorance.

Anne Hamilton
Brisbane, Australia 2020

1

Ancient Loyalties

Boxing Day
26 December 1960

THE INSIDE OF THE WARDROBE was dark and hot. But, at the back, behind the rack of coats and dresses, was a perfect hiding place. A little girl could cry her heart out in silent grief and, if she stayed as quiet as a mouse, no one would even know she was there.

But she wasn't alone.

A whisper, low and close, floated past her ear. 'If you concentrate hard enough,' said a voice, 'you can have anything you want.'

The little girl looked into her heart and knew that was true. So she put aside her pain and her shock and she concentrated. Minute after minute after minute went by. She focused intently, concentrating on building ever-increasing power in her mind. Minute after minute after minute went by. Still she concentrated. Then she stopped.

The little girl looked into her heart and knew she had enough power to move a range of mountains. *But...* 'This is silly,' she said. 'I'm leaving.' She brushed aside a coat.

'No!' The low, close whisper was edged with a very faint hint of anguish. 'You can't waste the power.' Its tone became more emphatic. 'You know it's *wrong to waste*.'

The little girl looked into her heart and agreed. She knew it was wrong to waste anything.

'Just think... you can have anything you want,' said the voice. 'What do you really, *really* want?'

The little girl looked into her heart and, suddenly, unexpectedly, she knew exactly what she wanted above all else. 'I want hell to move,' she answered.

She stepped out from behind the clothes. Shutting the door to the wardrobe, she also shut the door to her memory. And she didn't open it again for nearly forty years.

How an abnormally shy six-year-old comes up with the thought that what she wants above all else in life is for hell to move, I don't know. But I do know she did it. Because that little girl was me.

I discovered Christian fantasy in my early twenties and immediately fell head over heels for the genre. What was there not to like about *The Lion, the Witch and the Wardrobe*? It unfurled a flag of hope: 'The witch in the wardrobe,' it said, '*can* be defeated.' What a cup of refreshment that message was to my soul. I rushed to read the sequel.

But I was disappointed, crushed even. I loathed *Prince Caspian*. It took me decades to understand why I reacted so negatively: it was because the plotline raised the possibility the witch could be revived.

I was an appallingly shy child and young adult. Careful, cautious, hesitant. I might not have consciously known what the problem was, but my heart knew that a witch-spirit had tried to trap me and, in the process, had trapped itself. I was as much its jailer as I was mine. Because I had—somehow, who knows how?—used its name in my wish. And so I had tapped into the power of a name. It was the kind of mistake I was desperate not to repeat.

It was a fearfully depressing situation—and I'd never encountered anyone who'd even hinted there was a way out[2] until I read *The Chronicles of Narnia*.

But even with that glimmer of hope, the circumstances of life brought me to the edge of a dark pit. I was broken by depression and dispossession. Teetering on the edge of a complete breakdown, God caught me in mid-fall. Well, perhaps more accurately, He hit me with a lightning bolt. I felt as if some wild electrifying force flung me upwards and out of the pit just as I plunged over the edge. I've always felt, as a consequence, that I've never worked *through* depression. I've never done the hard tortuous yards of crawling up to the light. I was hurtled there by a beautiful passage in a children's book.

Yes, a Christian fantasy novel, but no, not any of *The Chronicles of Narnia*. Rather, it came from the writer who, more than any other, inspired CS Lewis' excursion into speculative fiction. Now I can tell you exactly what book and precisely what scene in that book changed my life. But I can't tell you why it made such an impact. Because you see, in my mental distress, I read the climax of *At the Back of the North Wind* totally in reverse. It took me years to realise I'd got it wrong.

George MacDonald's story is about a boy whose father is a coachman and has named him after his favourite horse. Diamond had a bed in the hayloft and it is there, through a hole in the wall, he comes to befriend the North Wind. Taken on adventures with this majestic Lady, he experiences gentle zephyrs, cold blustery gusts, and fierce, ship-wrecking gales. A deep desire begins to stir within him to go to the country at the back of the North Wind and when, at last, the Lady takes him to the North Pole, his opportunity arises:

> *He thought she must be dead at last. Her face was white as the snow, her eyes were blue as the air in the ice-cave, and her hair hung down straight, like icicles. She had on a greenish robe, like the colour in the hollows of a glacier seen from far off.*
>
> *He stood up before her, and gazed fearfully into her face for a few minutes before he ventured to speak. At length, with a great effort and a trembling voice, he faltered out—'North Wind!'*
>
> *'Well, child?' said the form, without lifting its head.*
>
> *'Are you ill, dear North Wind?'*
>
> *'No. I am waiting.'*
>
> *'What for?'*
>
> *'Till I'm wanted.'*
>
> *'You don't care for me any more,' said Diamond,*

almost crying now.

'Yes I do. Only I can't show it. All my love is down at the bottom of my heart. But I feel it bubbling there.'

'What do you want me to do next, dear North Wind?' said Diamond, wishing to show his love by being obedient.

'What do you want to do yourself?'

'I want to go into the country at your back.'

'Then you must go through me.'

'I don't know what you mean.'

'I mean just what I say. You must walk on as if I were an open door, and go right through me.'

'But that will hurt you.'

'Not in the least. It will hurt you, though.'

'I don't mind that, if you tell me to do it.'

'Do it,' said North Wind.

Diamond walked towards her instantly. When he reached her knees, he put out his hand to lay it on her, but nothing was there save an intense cold. He walked on. Then all grew white about him; and the cold stung him like fire. He walked on still, groping through the whiteness. It thickened about him. At last, it got into his heart, and he lost all sense. I would say that he fainted—only whereas in common faints all grows black about you, he felt swallowed up in whiteness. It was when he reached North Wind's heart that he fainted and fell. But as he fell, he rolled over the threshold, and it was thus that Diamond got to the back of the north wind.[3]

Somehow, where it says that Diamond would be hurt by walking through the door into the country at the back of the North Wind, I read into those words the exact opposite: that the North Wind would be hurt. That seemed impeccably logical to me. I saw the North Wind as a symbol of God and the door as an image of the cross, and so it made sense He would take the hurt onto Himself in Jesus.[4] The instant I came to this conclusion, some thunderbolt hit me. I was flung out of orbit and, when I picked myself up from wherever I'd landed, I found my entire emotional landscape had changed. I may not have got to 'the country at the back of the North Wind' but I was in a very much different place—a place on the other side of depression.

Now everyone's experience is different, but mine was that depression feels a lot like wandering in the land of the dead. Life and vitality are suppressed; a murky pall settles on all sides and it's impossible to make a choice because it looks like all of them are as gloomy as each other. Having got out of that wasteland, I've made brief visits back—but I've never taken up citizenship again.

Your problem may not be depression. But, as the Book of Job says, we're born to trouble as surely as sparks fly upwards. So, at some point in this book, I hope a heavenly arrow of lightning hits your heart, just as one zapped me so long ago. I pray that you realise the long, strong arm of Jesus reaches to the very bottom of the deepest pit of death and despair and that His superlative triumph over the troubles of this world—the aftermath of disease, disorder, drought, dispossession and every kind of darkness of mind and spirit—is just waiting to be effected in your life.

'Distress does not spring from the dust, and trouble does not sprout from the ground. Yet man is born to trouble as surely as sparks fly upward.'

Job 5:6–7 BSB

In the pages of Scripture, 'resheph' is mentioned seven times.[5] It is translated in various ways: *sparks, flames, arrows, thunderbolts, plague, inflammation, fever, hot coals, sirocco—the burning wind off the desert.*

There's no indication in these passages it is a pagan deity of deep antiquity. That aspect seems to have been virtually irrelevant as far as the prophets were concerned. Only two verses hint at Resheph having personal characteristics and at the possibility it may not be quite as inanimate as modern versions suggest. But it's easy to dismiss the main reference in Job 5:7 as poetic imagery—most translations don't pair *trouble* with the 'sons of Resheph' but with 'flying sparks'.

However, the extent of interaction between Jesus and Resheph is formidable. Jesus didn't treat it as impersonal, inconsequential or trivial. He didn't ignore it. On the contrary, He was so serious in His dealings with it I believe we should regard it with equal gravity.

Jesus engaged in nothing less than an all-out war against this particular spirit. In doing so, He fulfilled a long-expected role in an unexpected way. The Jewish people looked for the coming of the messiah—and, traditionally, it was thought there would be more than one saviour to liberate their nation. Stories spoke of the royal messiah, the 'Son of David', and the war messiah, the 'Son of Joseph'. No one really anticipated that these roles would be combined in one person, still less that the weapons of His warfare would be love and peace, healing and teaching.

It was only as I began to catch a glimpse of how, time after time, Jesus warred against the spirit of Resheph that I realised how prominent its role must have been across the ages. We miss so much of the magnificence of the victory Jesus achieved on our behalf because Resheph has been obscured and its significance in Israel's history has faded to the point of oblivion.

To rectify that situation, and so honour what Jesus accomplished on our behalf, we need to pick up the threads of a tapestry over three thousand years old. Back at that time—over a millennium before Jesus Himself was born—the tribe of Benjamin was the smallest in Israel. They had been almost completely wiped out in a civil war. At the end of the conflict, only six hundred men survived. No women. No children.

Centuries later, when Herod killed the infants of Bethlehem, Matthew quoted the prophecy of Jeremiah:

> *'A voice is heard in Ramah, mourning and great weeping, Rachel weeping for her children and refusing to be comforted, because they are no more.'*
>
> Jeremiah 31:15 NIV

The words of the Lord through Jeremiah could just as easily have applied to the past as to the future. The tribe descended from Benjamin truly were children of Rachel. As she lay dying, she had named him 'Ben-oni', *son of my sorrow*. Although her husband Jacob swiftly renamed him Benjamin, *son of my right hand*, Rachel's words were profoundly prophetic of what was yet-to-come in her younger son's bloodline. Deep, deep sorrow.

It may have taken hundreds of years for that grief to come to pass but, when it did, it was almost unimaginable. The only survivors of the genocide, the virtual extermination of the clan of Benjamin, were those few warriors who had managed to flee the final battle. Escaping to the Rock of Rimmon—a cave not far from the conflict zone, but still sufficiently far out in the wilderness to be safe—they'd holed up there for months.[6]

Now the adversary that pulverised Benjamin so thoroughly wasn't the Philistines or, for that matter, the Ammonites, Amalekites, Amorites, Moabites, Edomites or any of the other 'ites' who were the traditional enemies of Israel. Instead the adversary was the eleven other clans of the tribal brotherhood. For the moment, I intend to sideline the incident that set them all at each others' throats because much of that back-story features an entirely different threshold spirit. At present, I'd like to follow just a single line that involves and showcases the activity of Resheph. However, if you'd like to look further into that precipitating event at this stage, the story is told in detail in the last three chapters of the book of Judges.

In the aftermath of the civil war, the eleven tribes realised they had basically destroyed a brother in Israel and they were conscience-stricken. By annihilating nearly 98% of the men of Benjamin, not to mention all the women and children, the confederation of all the clans was wiped out. The brotherhood was irretrievably broken. And the obvious problem was that, without women, Benjamin could never be rebuilt. Normally, of course, it might be possible for the survivors to marry women from other tribes. However, the eleven had taken a solemn vow never to give up their daughters as wives to anyone from this clan.

The impasse was a formidable one. But then an opportunity presented itself. It was a horrific solution—but, still and all, it wasn't out of keeping with the atrocities already committed. The eleven tribes realised, on doing a head count, that no one from the city of Jabesh Gilead had responded to their call for war. It therefore occurred to the national leaders that, in punishing this city for its laxness, it was also possible to find a way through the impasse. So, off a battalion marched, destroyed the city and killed just about every one of the citizens. Only four hundred young girls were spared. They were then bundled off to be presented to the surviving men of Benjamin so the clan could be rebuilt and its territory repopulated.

So far, so disastrous. Those young girls who became the wives of the men of Benjamin and the mothers of their children were trophies of war. They'd been seriously traumatised; they'd lost everyone they loved and everything they held dear; they'd been taken captive and handed over to men who were very likely to have been mentally and emotionally disturbed by the massacre of nearly their entire tribe. Into this cauldron of strife, children and grandchildren are born. Are these little ones going to grow up mentally balanced? It doesn't take a degree in psychology to know the children would have been profoundly impacted by the brooding hatred, the desire for revenge and the intense bitterness that their entire community harboured towards outsiders. Particularly those they felt were to blame.

I have a theory I've mentioned quite often in my writing and speaking. It's immensely practical. In fact, it's so useful that I use it constantly in prayer ministry whenever I'm looking for clues about generational issues in a family—as well as the unique calling that covers a redeemed bloodline. My theory is this: parents have a very strong proclivity for naming their children in a way that highlights the unresolved spiritual problem of their ancestral line. Isaac and Rebekah, for example, named their second Jacob, *heel-grasper* or *deceiver*, for the ongoing issues of deceit in their family.[7]

So let's take a closer look at some names associated with the clan of Benjamin as it struggled to rebuild itself after this catastrophe.

> *Ner was the father of Kish, Kish the father of Saul, and Saul the father of Jonathan, Malki-Shua, Abinadab and Esh-Baal.*
>
> 1 Chronicles 9:39 NIV

> *Saul's sons were Jonathan, Ishvi and Malki-Shua. The name of his older daughter was Merab, and that of the younger was Michal.*
>
> 1 Samuel 14:49 NIV

Yes, the first king of Israel was born into this dire situation. As the Book of Samuel indicates, Saul wasn't exactly mentally stable. However, considering his generational line and the community in which he grew up, this should come as no surprise whatsoever. His raging jealousy was multi-faceted—yes, there were personal aspects to it but much of Saul's obsession with killing David was rooted in the ancestral feud between his hometown and that of Bethlehem.

When I was at university in the seventies, the conflagration known as 'The Troubles' was just beginning in Northern Ireland. My best friend at the time, third generation Australian of Irish descent, was able to pinpoint the real issue with unerring ease. Every time the subject came up for discussion, she steadfastly maintained it was Oliver Cromwell's fault. I didn't know enough about history to assess this notion but, one thing was quickly obvious, it was irrelevant that Cromwell was three centuries dead.

Since time immemorial, since the days of Eden in fact, we've had to have someone else to pin the blame on. For the tribe of Benjamin, it was natural to hold the people of Bethlehem responsible for all their woes. It's human nature that—regardless of our own participation in spiritual treachery—we don't want to stand, accused, and facing judgment. Especially naked and alone. We want to be able to point the finger and divert attention away from ourselves.

So the people of Benjamin looked to Bethlehem. Not only had the instigator of the civil war come from there, but sorrow had come forth from it since the day, centuries previously, when Rachel died at Bethlehem Ephrathah.

Saul's jealousy of David is the outward manifestation of his tribe's inner blight: the feelings of recrimination, animosity and menacing anger towards a long-dead perpetrator. Solomon, David's son, tells us:

> *Love is as strong as death, its jealousy as unrelenting as Sheol. Its sparks are fiery flames, the fiercest blaze of all.*

Song of Songs 8:6 BSB

In the Hebrew understanding of the Scriptures, there are four levels of interpretation.

- **Pashat** = *plain*, the obvious and surface meaning.
- **Remez** = *hint*, the deeper meaning; just beyond the literal.
- **Derash** = *inquiry*, the comparative, sifted meaning.
- **Sod** = *secret*, the meaning given through inspiration or revelation.

We're going to scratch beyond the surface of this verse in the last chapter of the Song of Songs. It's the beginning of one of the most touching and beautiful prophecies in the whole of Scripture and, to lift the veil on it, we need to look deeper.

Hidden within the Hebrew are:

- two direct references to Resheph: *sparks, flames*
- two allusions to Kish, the father of Saul—both through punning rhyme: *unrelenting, as Sheol*
- one indirect mention of Saul himself: *Sheol*

The only one even remotely obvious in English is Saul, which in Hebrew is Sha'ul, betraying its relationship to Sheol, often translated *hell*.[8] Sheol is the grave, the realm of the dead—in Hebrew conception, more fog than flames.

Now the combination of Saul and jealousy in the statement, *'Jealousy as unrelenting as Sheol,'* makes perfect sense in the light of the historical record. Saul was murderously jealous of David and, at the very end of his life, he wound up making a pact with Sheol. The presence of the name Kish makes sense too, since it's simply a father-son combination. But how does Resheph fit?

Kish is thought to mean *snaring*, *bird-catcher* or *bowman*. Curiously his name is believed to originate in Qos[9] or Qaus, a godling of the land of Edom who was depicted as an archer.[10] Like Qaus, the pagan deity Resheph was an archer. Both of them are portrayed holding thunderbolts aloft. We know exceedingly little about Qaus and only by comparison can it be said our information on Resheph is extensive.[11] Worshipped across a wide variety of cultures, including Egypt, Syria, the Hittite empire and Cyprus, Resheph is even recognised as being mentioned in Jain writings.[12] This godling was imaged as having the horns of a stag and its titles included:

- Lord of the garden
- Lord of the arrow
- Lord of thunder
- Gate-keeper of the underworld
- Door-warden of the sun
- Plague-bringer
- Healer

Those last two might seem contradictory but they simply recognise the fundamental nature of concentrated power. Power can harm and power can heal.[13]

Despite the widespread worship of Resheph,[14] it's generally acknowledged the name originates in the Hebrew language where it means *flame*, *lightning*, *burning coals*, *fiery arrows*, *plague* or *sirocco*. The common thought behind all of these diverse translations is *killing heat*. Whether we're struck by lightning, hit by flaming arrows, suffer sunstroke or need to be treated for the uncontrolled inflammation associated with an epidemic, 'resheph' is about heat intense enough to kill.

Some scholars hold the view that the most accurate interpretation of Resheph is *the scorcher*—the implacable, pitiless heat of drought or merciless fever.

So, as we go back to consider the verse, '*Love is as strong as death, its jealousy as unrelenting as Sheol. Its sparks are fiery flames, the fiercest blaze of all*,' we can see that as well as saying jealousy is a killer, it also indicates it brings devastating illness upon us—mental or physical. This was an abiding problem in the family line of Saul.

Jealousy is rooted in comparison. When we put ourselves or our possessions on the scales against those of someone else, our evaluation can lead to one of two outcomes: pride or jealousy. Either way we're in trouble: we've positioned ourselves to be consumed by Resheph or to receive retaliation from Leviathan.

Now this deeper level of interpretation of Song of Songs 8:6 raises an important question: what on earth was a man of Benjamin doing with a name like Kish? Perhaps it could be argued that it was about Yahweh. After all, for the Hebrew people, there was a genuine sense in which they perceived God as a divine archer: they saw His bow in the clouds and were puzzled by it. That was because the rainbow was pulled back so that the invisible arrow pointed mysteriously at His own heart. It wasn't until Jesus came that some of them started to understand God was willing to bear the wounds that would reconcile even His enemies to Himself.

But let's brush aside the ambiguity and recognise this as abandoning God. Just what inspired his mother or father to give Kish a name dedicated to a pagan deity— to no less than the Edomite equivalent of a ruler of the underworld?

What for that matter was Saul doing with a name so close to Sheol? Yes, certainly, his name means *desire* or *prayed for* and Samuel, on first meeting him, prophesied into that meaning.[15] But still, there's no escaping its links to the underworld.

The answers to those questions probably lie in the strong association between the people of Benjamin and the people of Edom from the southern desert beyond the Dead Sea. When Saul became king, he appointed Doeg the Edomite as his chief herdsman. At first sight, it might seem strange the first royal family chose someone entirely outside the clans of Israel for one of their most important officials. However, when we look at the names of Saul's kin, we realise there's much more to this alliance than is obvious on the surface. Several names amongst Saul's relatives are originally found amongst the chieftains descended from Esau—the twin brother of Jacob who was also called Seir, *hairy*, and Edom, *red*. In fact, Saul himself bears the same name as an ancient Edomite king.[16]

So what does this connection with the kingdom of Edom tell us? It says that, after the civil war, the people of Benjamin no longer looked to the tribal brotherhood for protection. Their trust was so completely shattered by the actions of the league they looked instead to outsiders beyond the remote borders of Israel. And they named their children for the kings and deities of those outsiders.

Names are harbingers of destiny. They are prophetic of calling. So, what were the people of Benjamin thinking? Were they playing at necromancy, the black art of communication with the dead? And if they were, then is it any wonder Saul was driven towards a final confrontation with the underworld when, on the night before he died, he visited the Witch of Endor and asked for the spirit of Samuel to be conjured up from Sheol?

It should be no surprise in all this to find that one of Saul's daughters—Michal—was also named for the underworld. Her name has several meanings[17] but one of them is identical to Mekal,[18] the patron deity of the Philistine city, Beth Shan.[19] Mekal is identified outside Israel as Resheph.[20]

Summing all this up, the unresolved problem in Saul's family line was a covenant with the underworld. Where did it start?[21] A clue exists within the name of his eldest son, Jonathan.

The darkness and defilement lying heavily on the first royal family of Israel was deep and intense. Yet God chose them! It's reassuring to know that, when we realise there's a yawning pit of iniquity in our family tree, God isn't going to use that as a reason to deprive us of our calling. Generation after generation in Saul's lineage were named after the lords of death and the underworld—not to curse them, though that was a natural consequence—but to prophesy to them they would be the ones to heal the pain of the past, to lift the nightmare of trauma, to restore darkness to light and to turn enmity to friendship.

In fact, Jonathan succeeded admirably at that last task. Saul paved the way for him and, actually, despite the scars on his own soul, accomplished a tremendous work of national healing. It's easy to underestimate how truly great Saul was. It's also easy to underestimate the enormity of the tragedy he created for the fledgling nation of Israel.

Jonathan, like the rest of his family, had been named for the unresolved spiritual issue in his bloodline. That was not just a covenant with the underworld but also an abiding generational hatred of a Levite named Jonathan.

Before looking into that back-story, let's take a moment to note one of the small items of circumstantial evidence that suggests Resheph is another name for Leviathan. Michal, Saul's daughter and incidentally the wife of Israel's second king, David of Bethlehem, was given a name equivalent to Resheph.[22] Her brother Jonathan on the other hand has a name directly linked to Leviathan. The element 'than' that occurs at the end of each name is *monster of the deep*.

Jonathan, blood-brother of David, is not the first of that name in Scripture. He's not even the second. There were ten men named Jonathan[23] in the Bible, including an uncle of David, a nephew of David and one of David's mighty men. However the first Jonathan on record was the grandson of Moses. His father, Gershom, was never high profile: we have very little of his story. We're told why he was named *foreigner*; we're told he was—apparently—present when Moses was attacked by God on the way to Egypt; and we're told he came with his mother, brother and grandfather to visit Moses at the camp in Sinai. Compared to his father, Gershom is almost invisible. Nonetheless, while Moses was barred from entering the Promised Land, it seems Gershom was not. In fact, there's a subtle and ambiguous hint in the Book of Judges that he settled in Bethlehem:

> *Now there was a young man from Bethlehem in Judah, of the family of Judah, who was a Levite; and he was **staying there**.*
>
> Judges 17:7 NASB

This young Levite is eventually identified as Jonathan, grandson of Moses. The Hebrew for *staying there* sounds like 'Gershom', so possibly this is a hint that he originally took up residence in Bethlehem. We don't know where Eliezer, Gershom's brother, settled but it may also have been in the vicinity.

Now Jonathan left his hometown of Bethlehem and headed up into the hill country belonging to the tribe of Ephraim. The reasons for his journey are not given but perhaps he was intending to visit his cousin, the high priest Eleazar. Now you may have noticed that Jonathan had an uncle Eliezer and a cousin Eleazar—and, yes, they are the same name. To foreshadow where this story, with all its twists and turns and intricate convolutions ultimately winds up, let me point out that, around a millennium and a half after this story takes place, the name Eleazar morphed into Lazarus.

The high priest, Eleazar, and his son Phinehas lived in the hill country of Ephraim. Now as I've pointed out through a lengthy comparison in *God's Priority*, I believe that Jonathan was jealous of Phinehas. In fact, insanely jealous would probably be a fair assessment.

> *Love is as strong as death, its jealousy as unrelenting as Sheol. Its sparks are fiery flames, the fiercest blaze of all.*
>
> Song of Songs 8:6 BSB

Here Solomon reveals that jealousy—the darkling shadow side of love—is empowered by Sheol and Resheph, the all-consuming spirits of the underworld. Jonathan allowed himself to fall for a temptation custom-designed for him. Passing by the homestead of a man named Micah, up in the hill country of Ephraim, Jonathan was offered an unusual position. Micah had fabricated a silver idol and an ephod—the breastplate of a high priest—no doubt basing it on Eleazar's apparel. He had then appointed his own son to perform sacrificial offerings and undertake divine inquiries for the family. But when Micah realised that his visitor was a real, live, genuine Levite, not to mention the grandson of Moses himself, he seized the opportunity and offered him a salary: an annual payment of ten silver pieces and a shirt.

A salary is about security. In accepting the position, the risks of receiving a tithe in an agricultural society were, for Jonathan, conveniently and completely bypassed.

So, Jonathan took the bribe. He became a private priest—for a single family, rather than a community. In addition, despite the fact he was not a descendent of Aaron, he adopted the garments of a high priest. He usurped the rights of Eleazar and later of Phinehas. As I said previously, I believe he was jealous of Phinehas—or perhaps more accurately of the extraordinary favour Phinehas had with God and the fame that had come his way when he'd stopped a plague.

Back on the far side of the Jordan, before entering the Promised Land, the Israelites had covenanted with Baal Peor through ritual prostitution and consuming food offered to idols. As a consequence, God had withdrawn His defensive cover. Plague had broken out; and Phinehas intervened to stop it.

Now by the time Jonathan dropped by Micah's place, decades later, the family of Moses had slipped into obscurity. We hear nothing, after all, of Gershom or his brother Eliezer. Instead we hear of the exploits of the national leader and war commander, Joshua. The family of Aaron nonetheless would still have retained a prominent place in all the various festivals throughout the year. But the family of Moses? They'd become virtually invisible.

I consider Jonathan to have been an ambitious man who chafed at the loss of prestige his family line had suffered. There's perhaps a hint of his covetous nature in the repeated mention of the silver—a curious Hebrew word, 'keseph', that derives from 'kasaph', *desire*, *greed* or *shame* with connotations of *being eclipsed*. Jonathan's employer, Micah,[24] certainly possessed an avaricious nature since he originally stole the silver from his mother and only gave it back because he was fearful of the curses he'd heard her pronounce on the thief. This may indicate she was practising 'kesheph', *sorcery*—not the same as 'keseph', *silver*,[25] but poetically close enough to imply more than the possibility.

Not long after Jonathan took the opportunity offered and settled into his role as Micah's tame priest, his domestic life took a turn for the worse. His concubine deserted him and went back to her father in Bethlehem. Many translations say she was unfaithful but the Hebrew text indicates she was angry. In our culture where divorce is commonplace, we often fail to catch the overtones here—it would have been extraordinary in those times for a woman to abandon her husband, go home and have the family actually accept her back. Whatever prompted her 'unfaithfulness' or 'anger' was unusual, to say the very least. Certainly it would have been an almost impossible situation—living with a man who had turned his back on all that a Levite was meant to represent to a community, who was flouting God's law and was ministering at a homemade shrine with an idol fashioned from cursed silver.

After a few months, Jonathan followed her down to Bethlehem, stayed several days at his father-in-law's home and wooed her back. Setting out late one afternoon with a servant in tow, Jonathan and his wife headed back to the hill country of Ephraim. They passed out of the territory of Judah and into the tribal lands of Benjamin. Deciding against seeking hospitality at the Jebusite fortress that was later to become Jerusalem, they kept going until nightfall.

Unfortunately for the travellers the town of Gibeah was an outpost of depravity. The residents were characterised as 'sons of Belial'. The incident that followed is a good example of how the threshold guardian, Belial, uses tactics including abuse and group mind control. Just as the travellers were sitting down for a meal, a contingent of citizens surrounded the house and demanded that the Levite be sent out so they could have sex with him. All sense of propriety was lost when the concubine was thrown to the wolves. Gang-raped all night, she lay dying as morning light approached. Her final action was to reach out and touch the sacred threshold stone in the doorway, accusing both her husband and the host of violating the covenant that should have protected her. They sacrificed her to save themselves when they should have sacrificed themselves to save her.

Jonathan then did something unspeakable: he cut up her body and sent the parts around the tribes as a call to war. The defilement he inflicted on the receiving tribes was immense: anyone who received this gruesome package and unwittingly touched the dead body would have had to purify themselves for a week. He intended to ensure a full gathering of the tribes through the shock value of such a grotesque gift and, in this, he succeeded. Everyone turned up—everyone, that is, except the men of Jabesh Gilead.

The end result was, as we've already noted, the almost total annihilation of the tribe of Benjamin as well as the slaying of all the citizens of Jabesh Gilead, barring the four hundred young girls taken off to rebuild Benjamin. After the war was over, Jonathan left Micah's service, stole the ephod and silver idol, and clandestinely headed off to the far north to start afresh. It was probably a wise move. The inter-tribal hatred he'd generated between Gibeah and Bethlehem was to go on for generations. His descendents, curiously, set up a golden calf up in the town where he eventually settled.

This repeat sin involving a golden calf is quite peculiar. Not peculiar in the sense it's a surprise that the lesson of the covenant violation at Mount Sinai hadn't been learned. Rather—peculiar in the sense that, if anyone set up a new golden calf, it should have been the descendants of Aaron. Generationally speaking, this defilement should have flowed down Aaron's lineage. Yet somehow it crossed over into the bloodline of Moses. In *God's Priority*, I pointed out that jealousy is the likely bridge that enabled this to happen.

The civil war with Benjamin resulted in fractures and wounds, feuds and hatreds that went on for centuries. It also resulted in enormous complicity with the angel principalities of other nations who wanted to occupy the land God had reserved for Himself. Besides Qaus of Edom, one of the spirits specifically—and frequently—named is Belial. In fact, it is clear there was an unholy alliance between the people of Gibeah and the spirit of Belial, since the men who wanted to rape the Levite were described as 'sons of Belial'. However, when considering the names in the family of Kish, with their dedication to the underworld, it becomes obvious that this pact with Belial, a demon of the wilderness, was possibly just one of many ungodly liaisons.

After all, just where did the covenant with the underworld originate? Was it after the war or before it? I believe the strongest indication is that it happened long before. I think that although the tribe Benjamin took the territory, they did little, if anything, to secure it spiritually. In my view, the covenant with the underworld emanated from the 'genii loci', *the spirits of the place*. Names in the general area seem to indicate dedications to denizens of the underworld. Two in particular stand out: Rimmon and Bethel.

Most translations suggest Saul was sitting under a pomegranate tree[26] when Jonathan began his two-man attack on the Philistines. One version, however, in line with Patrick Arnold's book on Gibeah, suggests that it was a cave which local Arab folklore still credits with being able to safely hide as many as six hundred men.

> *Saul was staying in the outskirts of Gibeah in the pomegranate cave at Migron. The people who were with him were about six hundred men.*

> 1 Samuel 14:2 ESV

According to Arnold,[27] this cave is pockmarked with cavities similar to the inside of a pomegranate. He identifies it as the Rock of Rimmon, *rock of the pomegranate*, the wilderness sanctuary where the six hundred survivors of Benjamin fled after the civil war.

Rimmon doesn't just mean *pomegranate*. It is the name of an Akkadian storm deity and forms part of the combination Hadad-rimmon, the location of a later battle on the plain of Megiddo where King Josiah was fatally wounded. Both Hadad and Rimmon were divinities of weather, both were connected to storms and both were linked to the underworld. Hadad was titled the 'cloud-rider', and was occasionally paired with Resheph. At the end of winter, Hadad's worshippers would stand outside a cave and call him forth from the underworld with ritual cries of: 'Where is the prince?'

The Rock of Rimmon is not the only location that hints at an underworld connection within the territory of Benjamin. Less than ten kilometres away[28] is Bethel, that famous town where Jacob had taken a stone for a pillow and had dreamed of angels ascending and descending on a stairway.

Effectively the 'pillow' was the threshold stone at the bottom of a flight of steps leading to heaven. Like the mercy seat on the Ark of the Covenant, it was the meeting place of heaven and earth. Jacob named the location 'Bethel', *the house of God*, because of his vision in the night. But its original Canaanite name was Luz, *almond*—another threshold symbol.[29] However the name Luz has another meaning: *twisted* or *deviant*. That is perhaps indicative of the 'crooked and perverse generation who lived there.'[30] In addition, Luz is poetically related to the name of the vampire and night demon, Lilith.

A new name doesn't displace the destiny of the old one. It simply adds another layer. Jerusalem is the prime example of this. Its ancient name Jebus, *dry*, *pain*, *persecution* and *walled-up*, reflects its present situation which incorporates the walled-off West Bank far, far better than the common epithet, *city of peace*. This principle—that a new name is simply not a replacement for the old, but a covering layer—means there's always the possibility of defilement from the past.[31] There's no automatic cleansing of the layers within our names just because we're believers. We have to go to God and ask for purification. God works via relationship, not via default settings. We therefore have to turn to Him and ask for our names—and their layers—to have their defilement removed.

Throughout its history, Bethel of Benjamin by no means always reflected its *house-of-God* tag. Whenever the prophet Hosea referred to it, he insisted on dubbing it Beth Aven—*house-of-evil*. And one of the most startling incidents of retaliation occurs in Bethel. Elisha went from Jericho to Bethel.

> *And while he was going up on the way, some small boys came out of the city and jeered at him, saying, 'Go up, you baldhead! Go up, you baldhead!' And he turned around, and when he saw them, he cursed them in the name of the Lord. And two she-bears came out of the woods and tore forty-two of the boys.*
>
> 2 Kings 2:23–24 ESV

I am indebted to the analysis of Arie Uittenbogaard who says that 'hair' in Scripture is symbolic of an intense awareness of God's wrath or revelation. By calling the prophet 'baldy', the boys were saying Elisha was completely without prophetic insight and therefore simply demented. With their cries of *'Go up! Go up!'* they were mocking his testimony to the ascension of Elijah and expressing their town's unbelief in the account; they were saying Elisha had either lied about what happened or else was mentally unhinged. They were basically demanding proof he had inherited Elijah's mantle by telling him to *'go up'* or ascend in a whirlwind, just as he claimed his mentor had done.[32]

Elisha cursed them for their dishonour. Retaliation was swift. In *Dealing with Leviathan*, the companion volume to this book, it's pointed out that the main legal right for the spirit of Leviathan to retaliate is dishonour. Assuming it's correct to identify Resheph as another name for Leviathan—and I believe it is—then it derives considerable legal power to restrain us from our destiny because of our dishonour.

A very similar example of dishonour inviting swift reprisal occurs in the story of Korah, a cousin of Moses and Aaron. Incensed—undoubtedly jealous—of the privileges given to his cousins by God, he confronted them:

> *'You have gone too far! The whole community is holy, every one of them, and the Lord is with them. Why then do you set yourselves above the Lord's assembly?'*

Numbers 16:3 NIV

Two hundred and fifty followers of Korah and his collaborators, Dathan and Abiram, came to the tabernacle door with censers, full of fire and incense. And there on the threshold, they were consumed[33] as the earth opened up and they descended untimely into Sheol, the underworld.

Abarim means *those who cross over*, with the implication that the place they are crossing over from is the underworld.[34] Korah, *bald*, might remind us of what the boys of Bethel called Elijah. However, in this case it is prophetically related to 'karah', *bargain* or *open up a pit*. Again, *pit* often implied *underworld*. Dathan, *decree* or *pit for a well*, mysteriously turns up a second time connected with jealousy—Dothan is the name of the place where Joseph's brothers threw him into a pit when they allowed their jealousy to take a murderous turn. Both names, Dothan and Dathan, contain 'than'—the element signifying *monster of the deep* and thus hinting of Leviathan.

As indicated in the previous book in this series, there are substantial implications flowing from Leviathan's role as a throne guardian within the divine royal court. One of these implications is that it is in charge of ensuring holiness and honour within that arena. These are the very things in contention—holiness and honour—during Korah's insurrection. '*The whole community is holy*,' he insisted as he and his fellow dissenters embarked on their ill-fated rebellion. With their censers, they acted as if the entire community had the right to act as priests and to stand within the earthly counterpart of God's throneroom: the Inner Court where the burning coals of the altar of incense are a sign of the holiness and purity of that place. Yet God had withdrawn that very privilege—the right of any man to be a priest for his own household and the right of the firstborn son to be the priest for the family—because of the worship of the golden calf. Instead He had given this honour to the Levites because they had sided with Him when Moses challenged the people to return to God.[35]

Korah, Dathan and Abiram were challenging God's right to judge and punish them. They dishonoured Him by refusing to accept His verdict: that the rights of priesthood were now restricted solely to the Levites until such time as God chose to decree otherwise. And that time was not in the foreseeable future. In fact, it didn't come about for well over a millennium—after and through the death of Jesus.

The swift retaliation experienced by Korah, Dathan and Abiram and their followers is not exceptional or singular.[36] Jeroboam, the first ruler of the Northern Kingdom after the split with the Kingdom of Judah, was rebuked by a man of God sent to Bethel to prophesy against the idolatrous altar that had been set up there. Turning on the man of God, Jeroboam raised one of his hands in defiance even while he was offering prayer and sacrifice. As he ordered the prophet's arrest, his hand instantly withered.[37] Stunned by the reprisal, he begged the man of God to intercede for him and, when the prophet did so, his hand was restored.

In the time of Isaiah, swift retaliation was also meted out to King Uzziah in remarkably similar circumstances.

What possessed Uzziah to decide to offer incense to God in the Inner Court is unclear. After all, he had the examples of Korah's rebellion and Saul's disobedience as warning. Perhaps his motive, as for Korah, it was jealousy. Or perhaps, like Saul, it was simply worry and distrust.

> *He waited seven days, the time set by Samuel; but Samuel did not come to Gilgal, and Saul's men began to scatter. So he said, 'Bring me the burnt offering and the fellowship offerings.' And Saul offered up the burnt offering. Just as he finished making the offering, Samuel arrived, and Saul went out to greet him.*
>
> 1 Samuel 13:8-10 NIV

Certainly the consequences for Saul were not as immediate or as dramatic as those for either Korah or Uzziah. However, Samuel informs him that, had he chosen otherwise—had he remained patient and trusted God—then his kingdom would been established for all time. As it was, it would pass to another; there would be no dynasty.

Uzziah, just like Korah, had a censer in his hand when his entire life was overturned by backlash for dishonour. He'd trespassed into the Inner Court of the Temple, a place reserved for Levites who had scrupulously purified themselves. Then he had gone up to the altar of incense to offer prayers. Some Levites courageously confronted him for this sacrilegious act and, as he was raging against them for daring to challenge him, they were astonished to see signs of leprosy break out on his face. He left the Temple precincts immediately but he never recovered and, for the rest of his life, the kingdom was governed by his son Jotham.

In his famous vision of the Lord's throneroom, Isaiah hints that the defilement of the sanctuary continued on even after Uzziah died. Until it was finally lifted, this uncleanness was also shared by both priests and people. The king's actions had personal repercussions for him both physically and spiritually, but there were national aftershocks too.

> *In the year that King Uzziah died, I saw the Lord, high and exalted, seated on a throne; and the train of His robe filled the temple. Above Him were seraphim, each with six wings... And they were calling to one another: 'Holy, holy, holy is the Lord Almighty; the whole earth is full of His glory.' ...*
>
> *'Woe to me!' I cried. 'I am ruined! For I am a man of unclean lips, and I live among a people of unclean lips, and my eyes have seen the King, the Lord Almighty.'*
>
> *Then one of the seraphim flew to me with a live coal in his hand... With it he touched my mouth and said, 'See, this has touched your lips; your guilt is taken away and your sin atoned for.'*
>
> Isaiah 6:1–7 NIV

One part of the office of a seraph is to ensure honour is maintained in the royal court. As I've pointed out in *Dealing with Leviathan,* I believe the evidence indicates Leviathan is a seraph and this explains why it retaliates so strongly against dishonour. When, as the priesthood of believers, we go into the courts of God to pray on behalf of others, we open ourselves to reprisal for any sort of uncleanness—but particularly dishonour.

We need to be very careful that our prayers are not presumptuous; that we are not dishonouring others while expecting favour for ourselves and that our attitude regarding our petitions is respectful and meek. It is the meek, as we know, who inherit the earth—and any prayer involving the overcoming of threshold spirits so we can enter into our calling is effectively a request to be granted our inheritance. All too often we take a stance that exudes power and authority, instead of grace-reliant humility. As a consequence, we find ourselves subject to retaliation from Resheph that we don't understand: killing heat—whether of drought or withering, fever or fire.

Isaiah had such grace-reliant humility. He saw the seraph bringing him a purifying coal from a heavenly altar—an action that paralleled and inverted Uzziah taking coals from an earthly altar to burn incense in a censer. The word for *coals* here is 'rizpah'—described by Brian Simmons as a *ceremonial stone* onto which incense was poured before being placed in the fire on the altar to produce an exquisite fragrance.[38] An alternative word for *coals* is 'resheph', which is related to 'seraph', *fire serpent* or *shining burning*.[39]

Resheph is therefore one of the seraphim. Like the cherubim, this class of angels are throne guardians who officiate as high functionaries within the divine court.[40] Resheph's position is confirmed in the prophecy of Habakkuk where he is described as one of the heavenly equerries who accompanies God as He journeys in from the sunrise:

> *Before Him went the pestilence, and burning coals went forth at His feet.*
>
> Habakkuk 3:5 KJV

Although it's not clear in many English translations with their tendency to remove any references to specific cosmic powers, there are two spirits named here. Often translators take the view that the prophet used a poetic device called personification and they erase the names, lest we think Deber, *pestilence*, and Resheph, *burning coals*, had personal identities and were not just 'things'.

However many scholars take the view that, with just a little wider context, it's fairly clear that *pestilence* and *burning coals* are not 'things' but 'beings'. So let's move our perspective out a couple of verses:

> *God came from Teman, and the Holy One from Mount Paran. Selah. His glory covered the heavens, and the earth was full of His praise.*
>
> *And His brightness was as the light; He had horns* [rays] *coming out of His hand: and there was the hiding of His power.*
>
> *Before Him went the pestilence, and burning coals went forth at His feet.*

Habakkuk 3:3–5 KJV

Now let's shift our viewpoint again to take in the very last speech Moses gave before his death—which, incidentally, was in the vicinity of Mount Abarim. First note that Teman is another name for Edom, and so too is Seir, and then look at how the words of Habukkuk amplify those of Moses:

> *The Lord came from Sinai and dawned over them from Seir; He shone forth from Mount Paran. He came with myriads of holy ones from the south, from His mountain slopes.*

> *Surely it is You who love the people; all the holy ones are in Your hand. At Your feet they all bow down, and from You receive instruction.*
>
> Deuteronomy 33:2–3 NIV

Deber, *pestilence*, and Resheph, *burning coals*, accompanied the myriads of holy angels who attend the Lord. They are at His command; they are His escorts, His high officials. When we revile them, we revile Him. Like Leviathan who retaliates against dishonour because that's part of its job profile, we see that Deber and Resheph have authorised positions in the royal court of God.

As I have repeatedly re-iterated in *Dealing with Leviathan*, one of the most common reasons people are smashed by spiritual retaliation is because they have dishonoured the high level cosmic entities called 'angelic majesties' by Jude and Peter in their epistles. These are fallen powers—but that does not give us the right or authority to dishonour them. Too many believers mistake the gift from Jesus of 'all authority' to mean that they can make their own rules, even rules contrary to Scriptural injunctions. Yet, what it truly means is that God has given us *His total backing to enforce and uphold His rules.*

When it comes to fallen 'angelic majesties', most of us are not much different to the tribe of Benjamin. We want revenge. Pure and simple. This desire comes out in our language about the satan, and sometimes in our actions towards him, revealing an interior attitude of spite and dishonour that God abhors. We're not called to honour the satan but we are instructed not to revile or curse, abuse or swear or insult him.

Our desire for revenge is strong. But we recognise we're so tiny by comparison to these formidable cosmic powers! So, like the clan of Benjamin, we look for more vulnerable targets in order to settle the score by taking out our vengeance on someone smaller and weaker than ourselves. Sometimes the retaliation we suffer at the claws of Leviathan is actually a blessing—because it immobilises us, stopping us from looking for some 'Gibeonites' on whom we can inflict harm. God sometimes allows severe, disabling retaliation so we will be effectively hindered from activating curses that will haunt our children, our children's children and our children's children's children as well. Like Joseph in Egypt, we should be able to say about the instigators of our troubles, whether they are human or spirit:

> *'You meant evil against me, but God meant it for good.'*
>
> Genesis 50:20 NASB

It isn't clear in Habakkuk's account whether Resheph and Deber are in rebellion against God. Resheph has definitely revolted but we can only infer that from how Jesus reacts to it. When it comes to spirits, our assumptions about their activities are often way off the mark. When something happens that we don't like—and that something has spiritual overtones—it's much easier to blame an evil spirit than it is to go to God and inquire if we truly are as innocent in the situation as we'd like to believe we are. Most of us are not Job—most of us are, in varying ways and to varying degrees, complicit with covenant-breaking. Even if that collusion is a passive settlement for the ungodly covenants our ancestors have raised, simply doing nothing active to repudiate them. Ironic and twisted as it seems, a pact with Leviathan gives it the right to retaliate against us for violating covenant with God. It can't honour an agreement with itself! Not for anyone who claims faithful allegiance to the Father from whom every family in heaven and on earth draws its name.

Our understanding of the spirit world is wracked with misconception. Michael Heiser carefully points out that the widespread Christian belief one-third of the angels fell in an insurrection against the Most High is nowhere mentioned in Scripture.[41] He also points out the passage from Habakkuk cited above contains the name of another pagan deity: Hby or Hebyon, *hiding one*.

I'm inclined to wonder if this spirit, allied as it seems to be with two of God's throne guardians, is the reason that, in spiritual warfare, we multiply demonic forces by naming more and more of them for their functions, while overlooking such significant entities as Resheph, Deber and the likes of Ziz, *spirit of forgetting*. I equally suspect Hebyon might be behind the almost complete erasure of Belial from most English translations in favour of the relatively innocuous descriptor, *worthless*.

A spirit with the single agenda of hiding others is such a clever way of keeping our 'eyes right'. I truly believe we've been misdirected when it comes to Resheph. The reason I think so is because, by my count, Jesus engaged with it at least seven times. Now it's obvious to me He warred against over seventy deities[42] at different times, but none of the others warranted the same level of attention as this lordling of stags.

Prayer

It is vitally important to recognise that prayer is about relationship with the Father. None of the prayers in this book are intended as a formula but as a guideline to help you realign yourself with the holy Trinity. They are meant as a starting point for a conversation.

Transformation is only possible as you hold onto the hem of Jesus' prayer shawl and ask Him to mediate before the Father for you. In the end, it's all about Him!

HEAVENLY FATHER, ABBA, DADDY GOD,

May I come into Your presence? I ask You to extend Your sceptre of favour to me. I am not deserving of it but I want to say I'm sorry. I have not known the difference between boldness and presumption, and sometimes I've crossed the line. You've asked me to be humble but I've been insolent. You've asked me to be patient but I've been demanding. You've asked me to be holy, but I've ignored the grace You offer to achieve it. You've wanted to lift me up but my disrespect has given Resheph the right to slap me down.

I repent of the many times I have stepped towards the threshold into my true calling, flaunting dishonour as I did. Resheph immediately blocked the way forward and I blamed You for not protecting me and my loved ones. Forgive me for dishonouring You in the first place and then doubling down on the dishonour by accusing You of abandoning my defence.

Forgive me for not taking responsibility for my own actions. Forgive me for further dishonouring You by believing it was You who caused my destiny malaise.

I stand before You to acknowledge that I have been reaping the fruit of the seeds of dishonour, jealousy and pride I sowed so long ago. I confess that it was my failure to honour You that has given Resheph the right to cause trouble in my life. I sincerely repent. Come, Lord Jesus, and empower the words of repentance I have just spoken. Come, Holy Spirit, and sweep away the ashes of dishonour in my life. Give me a vision of what honour of You looks like: a vision that shifts my understanding beyond my culture, my society, my family, my heritage. Empower me to fulfil that vision and honour You as I was created to, not as I think is right by my own standards.

Heavenly Father, Abba, I am sorry—truly sorry—and I ask Jesus to come as my Mediator and to wash my spirit, soul, heart and every part of me clean of all defilement caused by my dishonour. I ask Him to stand with me in Your heavenly court and present me to You as pure and undefiled.

Thank You, Jesus, for washing me clean of dishonour through Your blood. Thank You, Abba. Thank You, Jesus. Thank You, Holy Spirit. Amen.

2

Weeping for the Children

When Herod saw that he had been tricked by the magi, he became very enraged, and sent and slew all the male children who were in Bethlehem and in all its environs, from two years old and under, according to the time which he had ascertained from the magi. Then that which was spoken through Jeremiah the prophet was fulfilled, saying, 'A voice was heard in Ramah, weeping and great mourning, Rachel weeping for her children; and she refused to be comforted, because they were no more.'

Matthew 2:16–18 NASB

ECHOES OF THE ANCIENT FEUD between Bethlehem and Gibeah find their way even into the story of the birth of Jesus. Herod was an Idumean—that is, he was descended from the Edomites, the allies of the Benjaminites. And here in Matthew's gospel, we have that most peculiar square-peg-in-a-round-hole prophecy about Rachel, the mother of Benjamin, weeping for her children. How could the baby boys of Bethlehem be considered Rachel's children? They came from the tribe of Judah, not Benjamin. It seems like Matthew is stretching the words of Jeremiah an excessively long way to make them fit.

And yet, in Herod's insane jealousy—perhaps paranoia would be a better description, since the slaughter of the infants of Bethlehem was hardly an aberration, given he executed his first wife and three of his sons—we see reflections of Saul's madness. In Herod's desire to kill a younger king born in Bethlehem, we have a mirror into Saul's desire to do the same.

Perhaps the prophecy about Rachel refers to heartbreak over the sons of Benjamin who, no matter how many centuries have passed, still have not changed. Perhaps it's a lament that the jealous hatred between Saul and David was still evident over a millennium later, both in the tribe of Benjamin and in their allies.[43] History was repeating itself—and although both David and Jesus escaped the wrath of the reigning king, the innocents around them did not.[44] Just as Doeg the Edomite massacred the priests of Nob, so Herod the Idumean ordered the massacre of the boys of Bethlehem.

Curiously, both Doeg and Herod have names with similar overtones. Although Herod is said to mean *son of a hero* or *song of the hero*, to a Hebrew speaker, the name would have sounded like *coward* or *fearful*.[45] That is the root of the name Doeg, too—*fearful* or *anxious*.

Jealousy, madness, massacre, death: this ancient feud didn't stop in the first century. In the mid-nineteenth century, envious resentment—again centred on Bethlehem—led to the insanity of the Crimean War.[46] The precipitating incident involved the keys to the Church of the Nativity.

Such symptoms show the ascendancy of Resheph in our lives.

> *Love is as strong as death, its jealousy as unrelenting as Sheol. Its sparks are fiery flames* [resheph], *the fiercest blaze* [resheph] *of all.*

> Song of Songs 8:6 BSB

The relationship between Resheph and jealousy here recurs throughout Scripture. The fire that consumed Saul was intricately woven together with the unforgiveness in his community towards the people of Bethlehem—archetypally symbolised by the stone-slinging, giant-slaying, song-maker David.

And it didn't stop with either of their deaths.

When we fail to pardon others for their behaviour against us, we are inexorably drawn to repeat the very same actions we have judged as unforgiveable. It doesn't always happen: sometimes we find our failure to forgive means that the unforgiveable keeps repeating itself on our own heads instead.

> *Forgive us our sins, as we forgive those who sin against us.*

> Luke 11:4 NLT

Saul found himself in the first situation—that of failing to forgive. So he was tempted to commit the very thing he and his clan most hated: genocide. It was impossible for tiny, tiny, tiny Benjamin to attack Bethlehem with all the might of the tribe of Judah ready to repel them. But they could take it out on the Canaanite minority living in their midst.

The Gibeonites had tricked Joshua into a covenant hundreds of years previously. The fact that deception was involved was absolutely irrelevant to the status of the covenant. It was still in operation. The people of Israel were, under the terms of the covenant, required to defend the Gibeonites to the last man. Instead, Saul slaughtered them.

Long before the Scriptural record reveals this tragic covenant violation, it drops hints that something is amiss in Gibeon. As in *appallingly* amiss.

During the period after Saul's death, the kingdom was divided. For two years, the tribe of Judah followed David while the other clans looked to Saul's surviving son, Ish-bosheth. During this time, the armies of David and Ish-bosheth were out, roaming around the countryside, when they met up at Gibeon. They camped by the local Pool, one on each side, staring at each other across the water. Abner, the leader of Ish-bosheth's forces, suggested a bizarre game. He was apparently looking for a laugh, a bit of sport, a passing diversion. Joab, the leader of David's armies, agreed to the peculiar proposal Abner outlined.

Here it is: each side should choose twelve representatives and they should line up facing each other in pairs. Then they should grab each other by the hair and stab each other in the side with their swords.

Fun, right? More like demented. Not unnaturally, this game ended very badly. Very, very badly. All the players died. After which, it's almost as if the armies wake from a trance and, realising their friends have just been killed, attack each other. Abner escaped the battle but put a spear through Joab's brother—setting the scene for a later episode of trickery and revenge. David then condemned Joab for seeking vengeance and praised Abner. Arie Uittenbogaard comments: 'David's response, the bizarreness of the suicide sacrifice of the twenty-four soldiers and the numerical significances pertaining to these events seem to suggest that this story has more than one meaning, and the true gist of it escapes the casual reader.'[47]

I couldn't agree more. However, the casual reader should still become aware that something is very seriously wrong at Gibeon. What kind of spirit was operating there that twelve pairs of men were sent to their deaths just for the fun of it? In fact, although Resheph, spirit of the underworld, certainly was the beneficiary of this threshold game, it was Belial, the spirit of armies, of perversity and of group mind control—all evident in the story—who inspired this murderous pastime.

It is another nineteen chapters before the chronicle reveals what happened at Gibeon to cause Belial—and the vampire spirit, Lilith,[48] as well—to take up residence there. Only when David sought the Lord about a devastating famine was the massacre of the Canaanite minority revealed.

> *During the reign of David, there was a famine for three successive years; so David sought the face of the Lord. The Lord said, 'It is on account of*

Saul and his blood-stained house; it is because he put the Gibeonites to death.'

2 Samuel 21:1 NIV

Saul's covenant violation is easy to denounce and David's covenant-keeping easy to esteem. Except it's not that simple. Both men are complex and contradictory: David eventually succumbed to temptation and wound up breaking covenant, while Saul accomplished a great work of national reconciliation. Let's not forget Saul was up against the odds—his family were part of a covenant-breaking community while David's family was descended from famous covenant-keepers: Rahab and Salmon, along with Ruth and Boaz. Saul's praiseworthy achievements tend to be very greatly overshadowed by his deep faults. In the wake of the destruction of the clan of Benjamin, the first king—no matter who he was—had an immense calling on his life. His destiny was to reunite the tribal brotherhood. Whether he achieved that destiny or not, depended on three critical conditions—tests, in fact—that were the necessary precursors, spiritually speaking, to national healing:

(1) reconciling the people of Benjamin with a priest from the hill country of Ephraim

(2) reconciling the people of Israel with the people of the town of Jabesh Gilead

(3) reconciling the people of Gibeah with the people of Bethlehem

Amazingly, despite the scars on his soul coming down from his ancestors, Saul brought about the first two of these. That's a staggering accomplishment when we remember he was subject to black moods and massive depression—which, at least in part, were a legacy of his father's line surviving a genocide and his mother's line being a trophy of war.

His friendship with Samuel, who came originally from the hill country of Ephraim, is the means by which Saul achieves the first reconciliation.[49]

His first action as king—saving the people of the resettled town of Jabesh Gilead—is the means by which he achieves the second reconciliation.

However, on being faced with a shepherd boy from Bethlehem who could play the harp like an angel, slay six-fingered giants and inspire unswerving loyalty even within Saul's own family, all the latent generational hatred in his bloodline came to the fore.

Jealousy is the final ordeal that the spirit of Python flings at us as it leaves. Python is a threshold guardian with a legitimate right to test all of our choices and it piles on enormous pressure to push us back from our calling. The wily manoeuvres it attempts in order to induce us to choose unwisely include constriction, silence, divination, intimidation, flattery, seduction, illness.[50] But when it becomes apparent it is losing, then it leaves—but not without setting in place one last defilement: the temptation to jealousy. This is Python's cry for reinforcements—for help from Leviathan, so that we can be whipped back across the threshold and deprived of our calling, even as we've achieved finally it.

This was Saul's story. He lost his calling. He started exceptionally well—making superb choices that brought great healing into the tribal confederation through upending the rifts of the past. He became the go-between who reconciled the people of Jabesh Gilead with the nation, and he also became the bridge-builder who restored the relationship of his own community with the priests of the hill country of Ephraim. But Python finally found a weak spot, and Saul's jealousy of David was his undoing.

His inability to pass the third test had immense ramifications. Instead of 'mending the world' by reconciling the people of his hometown with the people of Bethlehem, he multiplied the curse and sent it hurtling down his generational stream. If he'd kept covenant with David, as his own son did, further tragedy might have been avoided. Had he been able to forgive the people of Bethlehem, the root of bitterness would have been uprooted—but instead it defiled his judgment and the Gibeonite massacre occurred.

Saul's failure to keep covenant with the Gibeonites wasn't simply a personal failing—because he held the office of an anointed king, it was a governmental failure as well. This is why, in a later time, David faced the exactly same issue.

Yet, for David, the confrontation came with a dark twist. It pitted one covenant against another. David was faced with famine after three years of unremitting drought—the *killing heat* symptomatic of the activity of Resheph.

Like Leviathan, the primary legal right Resheph invokes to exercise its power in the world is dishonour. In this situation, Saul had not only dishonoured the Gibeonites, he'd dishonoured the Lord who required the covenant to be kept. David had a chance to mend the mess Saul had created, but he too failed. He'd racked it all up into an even bigger disaster. When he went to the Gibeonites and asked them what they wanted as recompense, they'd made it clear they wanted revenge. In the usual eye-for-an-eye manner, they wanted to wipe out the house of Saul—and they wanted to do so as part of a sacrificial ritual at the start of the barley harvest.

David agreed. He must have been truly desperate. Attempting to solve Saul's covenant breach by making another covenant breach is not a fix. David amplified the problem. He had a covenant with Saul, since he was the king's armour-bearer.[51] But, irrespective of that covenant, he had one with Jonathan involving an exchange of mantle and weapons:

> *Then Jonathan made a covenant with David because he loved him as himself. And Jonathan removed the robe he was wearing and gave it to David, along with his tunic, his sword, his bow, and his belt.*
>
> 1 Samuel 18:3–4 BSB

These gifts from Jonathan to David are not mere souvenirs of the covenant ceremony. The robe is a call to faithfulness and symbolises adoption into the family. The weapons signify a vow to always defend the other, even unto death. The whole rite means: 'You and I are one. We have exchanged inheritances. We are now blood brothers; we're part of each other's family; if one is attacked, the other will rush to his aid; if one is killed, the other will protect and care for the bereaved family as long as he lives. This covenant is binding on our descendants; our families are united forever.'

Jonathan's gift was immense: he effectively abdicated as crown prince, confirming David as the next king. The weapons he gave David were great prizes: out of all the people of Israel, only Saul and Jonathan had metal armaments.

Some time after Saul and Jonathan had died in battle, David asked: *'Is there still anyone left of the house of Saul, that I may show him kindness for Jonathan's sake?'*[52] That question indicates David's integrity in faithfully remembering his covenant with Jonathan. That covenant covered the entire House of Saul and still required David to defend them to the death.

Yes, this covenant *alone* put all of the surviving members of Saul's line under David's protection. Add to it the covenant he had with Saul himself and David was doubly obligated to shield the remaining members of the first royal family from all harm. So when the Gibeonites asked for revenge, he should have pointed out they wanted him to rectify a covenant violation by making another covenant violation. *Sorry*, he should have said. *Choose something else.*

But he was desperate. More than that, he was undoubtedly tempted. He had the opportunity to remove every viable, legitimate contender for the throne from the former dynasty in one fell swoop. Furthermore, he had a politically acceptable reason for breaking his well-known covenant with the House of Saul. No one would question it: the lives of seven people or the lives of thousands. In saving the nation from the famine, he also could secure the kingship for his lifetime—and beyond.

Whatever his motives, David did the unthinkable. He broke covenant and handed over seven men from the House of Saul to the Gibeonites. Perhaps once again the Gibeonites had exercised remarkable trickery: with Joshua, they wanted covenant; with David, the breaking of covenant. Neither leader consulted God. I think we can say this with surety despite the silence of the record regarding David, since I believe God would have directed him to negotiate an outcome combining both justice and mercy as well as keeping covenant.

So the seven men were killed and their bodies exposed, thus cursing and defiling the land.[53] In a culture where respect for the dead required same-day burial, exposure to the elements was the supreme disgrace. The Gibeonites had lived for centuries amongst the Israelites: they *intended* to dishonour both king and country, to heap shame on the God of the Covenant. The Philistines had exposed the bodies of Saul and his sons on the walls of Beth Shan partly for this reason: to heap dishonour on them and on the Israelites.

David didn't fix the problem regarding the famine. He made it worse. He poured oil on the flames of dishonour. He heated the furnace higher—granting Resheph even more extensive rights.

But then... oh, *but then*... God, in His mercy, allowed a voice of conscience to emerge. In the matter of Bathsheba and Uriah, it was Nathan who confronted David with a parable about a man and his lamb.[54] In the matter of the Gibeonites, David's honour was re-awakened by a woman. Her name was Rizpah and she was Saul's concubine. Generally speaking, a concubine was a minor wife—often a cousin married to ensure an inheritance of land remained within the confines of the family.

Rizpah means the same as Resheph, *burning coals*. Her name is found in Isaiah's description of heaven's throneroom when a seraph brings down a *coal* to purify his unclean lips. Rizpah's father was Aiah, meaning *falcon* or *desire*. It's another name from Edom[55] and within it are contradictory overtones of both *jackal* and *Yahweh*. In fact, one possible interpretation is: *where is God?* Here we see the cry of every heart during inexplicable tragedy: 'Where is God in all this?' So, yet again, in these two names—Rizpah and Aiah—we see the tension in the clan of Benjamin regarding spiritual allegiance. On the surface, Rizpah and Aiah point to the Lord God but, not too far below it, there's a subtle whiff of the underworld.

> *Then Saul's concubine Rizpah, the daughter of Aiah, used sackcloth to make a shelter for herself on the rock where the corpses were, and she stayed there from the beginning of harvest until the autumn rains came. During the day she would keep the birds away from the corpses, and at night she would protect them from wild animals.*
>
> 2 Samuel 21:10 GNT

Since the men were killed around the Passover—March or April—and the autumn rains don't arrive until October or November, this was around six months! In the Hebrew it's actually unclear when the rain finally arrived but, assuming it was in the normal cycle, then half a year is quite reasonable. The drought didn't break at once. The searing heat of summer still had to be endured. Resheph the scorcher was still ascendant.

Rizpah's action caught the attention of the nation. Grief-stricken, bereft, she tried to protect the last tatters of honour for a family unspeakably dishonoured. Rizpah doesn't just mean *burning coals*: it also means *joined tiles*.[56] Significantly, so does Resheph. However, *joined tiles* is evocative of the impenetrable joined scales so significant to the name Leviathan, *joined sea monster*—and, of course, to Levi, *joined.*

Saul had been called to unite the nation after the civil war, but it was his concubine who actually joined the pieces back together by awakening David's conscience.

On a complete tangent, I wonder what ancient people thought of tiling. Was it a sacred art? It must have had some major significance, since the sword-bearing tiler—or tyler—of the Masonic Lodge is a traditional threshold guardian. The tiler's sword might be decorative today but that wasn't the case in the past. Moreover the checkerboard floor, which is one of Freemasonry's most recognised symbols, represents the ground floor of Solomon's Temple—thereby suggesting that tiling is indeed bound up with concepts like Levi and joining; the priesthood and the Inner Court; Leviathan and the royal court of heaven; 'rizpah' and 'resheph' and the burning coals of the altar of incense. It's all about the consecrated space in which the glory of God—His honour—will not be compromised.

And that's what David finally woke up to: the nation's spiritual morass was all about honour. Honour of God. Honour of covenant.

Psalm 7 begins with the words:

> *I come to You for protection, O Lord my God. Save me from my persecutors—rescue me!*

> Psalm 7:1 NLT

This song is prefaced with a strange dedication: '*A Shiggaion of David, which he sang to the Lord concerning Cush, a Benjaminite.*'

Who on earth is Cush? As Jewish scholars point out, there is no other mention of a Cush from the tribe of Benjamin anywhere in Scripture. They propose it to be an almost-certain reference to Saul—but I think it's far more likely to point to his father, Kish.[57] In another instance where the word 'Cush' appears, the ancient translators of the Septuagint[58] rendered it as *scorched face*.[59] And although Kish doesn't mean *scorched*, Resheph has precisely that overtone—thus suggesting that the link I've made between Kish, the Edomite deity Qaus and the Syrian godling Resheph is a valid one. David's use of 'Cush' may possibly be a way of alluding to one of the godlings of the nations without actually mentioning its proper name.

Now 'shiggaion' is an unusual word, often suggested as an instruction to the musician. However it is related to words for *to misjudge* or *make a mistake*. I differ from Jewish commentators who think David's mistake was to rejoice at Saul's death or else to cut off a corner of his robe when Saul was relieving himself in a cave and didn't know David was hiding there.[60]

I believe that David finally realised he had made a terrible mistake in not keeping his covenant obligations to the family descended from Kish. Far too late, he regretted handing over the sons of Saul to the Gibeonites. His plea for God's protection, his declaration that he did what he did with good intent and integrity, and his mention of 'flaming arrows' could well allude to Resheph and also to any criticism he encountered from his own people. While the drought continued, there'd have been public mutterings about David's action. People would have questioned his wisdom in violating his own well-known covenantal obligations to bring an end to the devastating consequences of another broken covenant. David's thinking had somehow been twisted: very similar to the way Leviathan twists communication.

Pragmatically speaking, there's no doubt that, if David's action in handing over the seven members of the House of Saul had worked and the famine had ended immediately, there'd have been nothing but praise. He'd have saved the nation, just like Joseph had done in Egypt.

But if Rizpah was on that hill for six months? No. That was a public relations disaster. Moreover, spiritually speaking, the dishonour for covenant breach was multiplying the whole time. The cycle of genocide could easily have started again, but for God's mercy and David's contrite heart. Because—finally—his conscience pricked by Rizpah's action, he did wake up to what had happened and the mistake he'd made. He then ordered the bones of the men to be collected from the hilltop and he sent for the bones of Saul and Jonathan from Jabesh Gilead. Then, gathering them all up, he had them buried honourably and with appropriate mourning in the tomb of Kish, not far outside Jerusalem. And then—*then*, not before—God answered prayer on behalf of the land.

Then. When honour had at last been restored.

Saul and Jonathan had been initially buried at Jabesh Gilead. This town, on the eastern bank of the Jordan River within the tribal territory of Manasseh, is undeservedly obscure. Wadi Al-Yabis in the present-day Hashemite Kingdom of Jordan is believed to be named after it and, while the ruins of the city have not been positively identified, there are several strong candidates in the vicinity. In later centuries, Jabesh Gilead is thought to have been renamed Tishbe. Thus it is considered to be the birthplace of the prophet Elijah.

Wadi Al-Yabis itself is thought to be the ravine of the Brook Cherith, famed as the place where Elijah was fed by ravens.[61] The seasonal stream here flows into the Jordan almost directly opposite the ancient locations of Salim and Aenon, where John the Baptist moved later in his ministry in order to have plenty of water. The pools of Wadi Al-Yabis therefore seem to have been John's original baptismal site at Bethany-beyond-the-Jordan, until such times as they dried up.[62] Much as they did in the time of Elijah.

John the Baptist was, as Jesus said, the prophesied Elijah-who-was-to-come who would turn the hearts of the children to their fathers and the hearts of the fathers to their children. So what better way to identify himself than by ministering in the very environs so steeped in the traditions of Elijah?

It was here, in Bethany-beyond-the-Jordan, that John baptised Jesus. Where the ravens had come in the time of Elijah, a dove descended. It was from this place, in Bethany-beyond-the-Jordan, that Jesus was driven out into the wilderness by the Holy Spirit. And it was here He returned, much later in His ministry, when His life was threatened after He'd healed the man born blind. At that point, in the last winter of His life, He retreated with His disciples to the place where He'd met the first of them—in Bethany-beyond-the-Jordan. Jesus was not the first to seek refuge here, nor was He the last. Elijah had also had a hideout in this spot and, in the latter half of the first century, the early Christians chose to flee to this region when they saw the armies of Rome surrounding Jerusalem.

But most importantly, for our study of Resheph, it was here, in Bethany-beyond-the-Jordan, that Jesus received the news of Lazarus' illness.

In summary—looking forward from the time of David—Jabesh Gilead was to become, in later ages, weighted down with immensely rich historical significance. In David's time, it was famous for both the faithlessness of its citizens and, contrariwise, also for their faithfulness. It was a town in which dishonour and reprisal were almost woven into its DNA—until it come to exemplify exactly the opposite. Both Leviathan and Resheph are found hiding in its background story—and yet, when they are overcome through honour and through the work of Jesus—it became a refuge of peace.

In fact, it may well be the famous 'Refuge in Edom' prophesied by Daniel,[63] since that promised sanctuary included not just Edom but also Moab and Ammon—and Jabesh was in the ancient territory of the Ammonites.

Now the first time anything noteworthy is heard about Jabesh Gilead in Scripture was when its citizens failed to attend the muster of the tribes during the civil war against Benjamin. In a partly punitive measure and partly as an opportunistic way around the vows they'd come to regret, the tribes sent in an elite force to destroy the town and kill everyone. Everyone, that is, except for those four hundred girls who were handed over to the Benjaminites.

The second time anything noteworthy is heard about Jabesh Gilead was a generation or two later. The town had been re-settled and had come under attack by the Ammonite king, Nahash. The populace agreed to surrender, but not unconditionally—they wanted a treaty. Nahash, however, had a stipulation:

> *'On this condition I will make a treaty with you, that I gouge out all your right eyes, and thus bring disgrace on all Israel.'*
>
> *The elders of Jabesh said to him, 'Give us seven days' respite that we may send messengers through all the territory of Israel. Then, if there is no one to save us, we will give ourselves up to you.'*
>
> 1 Samuel 11:2-3 ESV

Nahash, as I've pointed out in *Dealing with Leviathan*, is a variant spelling of 'nachash', *serpent*, and is the very word that Isaiah used in his prophecy to describe Leviathan. It's also a word associated with smelting copper and bronze.[64] It is no surprise that King Nahash wanted to bring disgrace and shame on all Israel, because in overcoming the spirit of Leviathan, honour and dishonour are the very issues at stake.

The desperate people of Jabesh found an unexpected champion. Perhaps they thought, given their town's history, that there would be no help from outside—after all, the previous inhabitants had refrained from helping others. Certainly King Nahash seems to have expected that the townspeople would be abandoned to their fate. He was counting on disgracing not just the men of Jabesh but the entire nation.

Yet a descendant of one of the young girls abducted from Jabesh came to their rescue: Saul of Benjamin. It was his first act as king of Israel—and it brought a large measure of healing to the ruptured tribal brotherhood.

Honour and dishonour thread their way through this narrative. The Jewish historian Josephus[65] suggests that Nahash's threat of blinding the men of Jabesh wasn't an idle one, and that he had inflicted it on the residents of other cities. It was utterly ruthless but totally logical; Nahash was making sure his territorial conquests were secure by maiming the men who surrendered so that they could not later rebel against him.

The people of Jabesh were incredibly thankful to Saul for his intervention in saving him. They would, they said, be eternally grateful. It's one thing to say it; but it's another to back the words with actions. Nevertheless they were eventually to put their lives on the line just to keep their word in this regard. Years went by, decades in fact, and Saul and Jonathan were both killed on Mount Gilboa. The Philistines celebrated this major victory by stripping Saul's body of his armour and dedicating the spoil to their war goddess, Ashtoreth. Then they fastened his corpse, along with the bodies of his sons, to the wall of the citadel of Beth Shan.

> *When the Philistines came to strip the dead, they found Saul and his three sons fallen on Mount Gilboa. They cut off his head and stripped off his armour, and they sent messengers throughout the land of the Philistines to proclaim the news in the*

temple of their idols and among their people. They put his armour in the temple of the Ashtoreths and fastened his body to the wall of Beth Shan.

When the people of Jabesh Gilead heard what the Philistines had done to Saul, all their valiant men marched through the night to Beth Shan. They took down the bodies of Saul and his sons from the wall of Beth Shan and went to Jabesh, where they burned them. Then they took their bones and buried them under a tamarisk tree at Jabesh, and they fasted seven days.

1 Samuel 31:8–13 NIV

Now it wouldn't have been particularly difficult for the news to reach Jabesh Gilead of the Philistine celebration and their despoliation of the bodies of Saul and his sons. The heights of Wadi Al-Yabis actually overlook the walls of Beth Shan on the opposite bank of the Jordan. An eagle-eyed sentry could have deduced what had happened from observing the festivities in the Philistine city.

So the men of Jabesh made a plan. A group of their best warriors travelled all night, crossed the Jordan and made their way to Beth Shan. Taking down the bodies under cover of darkness, they brought them back to Jabesh, burned them and buried the bones under a tamarisk tree. Then, because they'd touched dead bodies, they followed the Law, separated themselves, and fasted for seven days.

The lengths they went to in order to keep their word—given forty years previously—and to display honour towards Saul probably bought time, spiritually speaking, for the nation of Israel. They postponed an inevitable retribution; but they couldn't avert it.

The mention of the tamarisk tree is significant. Although it is unclear what the symbolism of a tamarisk is in Scripture, in the wider Mesopotamian region it represented exorcism.[66] It was about expelling evil spirits.

Did the men of Jabesh know Saul had visited the Witch of Endor on the night before the final battle? Did they know she had—to her own surprise—summoned Samuel up from Sheol and he'd prophesied Saul would be with him in the underworld within a day? Probably not. Probably they were thinking about the despoliation of the bodies and the dedication of armour to the patron deities of Beth Shan. Scripture mentions Ashtoreth but archaeology points to Mekal—spelled, it would appear, the same way as Michal, Saul's daughter.[67] Mekal is elsewhere identified as Resheph.[68]

It doesn't matter how we parse this situation, it's clear that—in the hours leading up to his death as well as in its aftermath—the godlings of the underworld made their final claim on Saul. In many respects, that claim had been there all his life—it had come with his name. But on that last day, with God hiding His face, the very last thing Saul ever needed to do was break his own law, consult with a medium, and look for advice from the underworld.

When David sent for the bones of Saul and Jonathan, he began a work of honour and restoration that was only finished a millennium later when Jesus took a hand in it.

So often that's our situation too. We are called to begin works of world-mending only Jesus can complete. But the fact we cannot complete them ourselves is no excuse not to begin. As Rabbi Tarfon so aptly said: 'It is not your responsibility to finish the work of perfecting the world, but you are not free to desist from it either.'

Back in the early 1980s, I was asked to organise a small conference. I'd never done anything like that before, so I pleased to be given a list of explicit instructions. I was told to send an invitation to a particular speaker whose name, unfortunately, I no longer recall. However I do remember the topic I was told to ask him to speak on. It was: *Glory*.

It's different now, but back in those days, no one even thought about *glory*, let alone talked about it. Still, I imagined that this lecturer would expound on Isaiah's vision of God with His train filling the temple or perhaps the encounter of Moses with God at the burning bush. Or maybe it would be the Transfiguration, one of my favourite stories about Jesus. My mind was full of glowing, effulgent clouds and dazzling pyrotechnics.

But no.

The speaker, over several sessions, kept exploring Saul's relationship with the people of Jabesh Gilead. I have to say I was puzzled. Moreover, I remained so for many years. I just didn't get it. How on earth did this story exemplify *glory*?

Now, decades later, I consider it the most pivotal story in all of Scripture. Okay, maybe on second thoughts, the Transfiguration nudges it out of top spot but nevertheless it's still right up there. I can now see the mutual honour exchanged between Saul and the people of Jabesh at the beginning of his reign healed both land

and people. In addition, that healing created a safe haven where people could seek refuge—it created a valley of such deep *shalom* that, in the following millennium, it became the go-to sanctuary for a wide variety of people. As I mentioned previously, Elijah hid out there; John the Baptist started his ministry there at Bethany-beyond-the-Jordan; Jesus was baptised there; the early Christian community, seeing the Roman legions surrounding Jerusalem, heeded the words of Jesus and fled there.[69]

In fact, Jesus Himself in the last winter of His life took refuge there. How did the people of Jabesh Gilead turn their wounded land into a cloister of peace and a nest of glory? Very simple. They honoured the king. In a later age, the apostle Peter said:

> *Show proper respect to everyone, love the family of believers, fear God, honour the emperor.*
>
> 1 Peter 2:17 NIV

This was no easy ask in those days. Peter was quite possibly talking about Nero. Now certainly Peter didn't mean *worship* the emperor; he meant to give due *respect*. Jesus had said:

> *Render to Caesar the things that are Caesar's, and to God the things that are God's.*
>
> Mark 12:17 ESV

The people of Jabesh Gilead did what they could to honour Saul, even in death. David sang a lament but, when he finally had sufficient support to receive the throne—as an indirect result of an argument over Rizpah, Saul's concubine—he did nothing more. It was a long and august tradition to honour the leaders of the people at their deaths with national mourning. But it didn't happen—at least, not until Rizpah (again!) who, as a woman of Benjamin, was almost certainly a descendant of the girls abducted from Jabesh Gilead, awoke David's moral conscience. His actions—in allowing the Gibeonites to defile the slain bodies of Saul's family—were a stark contrast with those of the men of Jabesh Gilead who'd done all they could to lift the Philistine defilement on the slain bodies of other members of Saul's family.

David acted dishonourably. *Honour* is incredibly important to God. It is His *glory*. They are the same word in Hebrew. When we speak ill of our leaders, even those who are deceased, we send His glory away and bring drought on our land. It wasn't just Saul's actions that caused the spiritual problem; David compounded the issue. When it comes to our own nation, God isn't going to answer prayer to heal our land, just so we can abuse His grace by continuing to dishonour those in authority over us.

The original name of Jerusalem was Jebus, which has the same meaning as Jabesh. Basically they both mean *dry*, but they also evoke the notion of *withered up* or *ashamed*. Additionally they mean *pain*, *affliction* or *persecution* and resonate with the idea of being *walled-up*. Another name that has all these overtones is 'Jabez'.

> *Now Jabez was more honourable than his brothers, and his mother called his name Jabez, saying, 'Because I bore him in pain.' And Jabez called on the God of Israel saying, 'Oh, that You would bless me indeed, and enlarge my territory, that Your hand would be with me, and that You*

would keep me from evil, that I may not cause pain!' So God granted him what he requested.

1 Chronicles 4:9–10 NKJV

Jabez, like David, was from the clans of Judah. He probably got his name because he was in the breech position within his mother's womb. Being effectively walled-in, he caused his mother great distress during the birthing process. As he grew up, he was conscious of the power of a name to affect his destiny—he would constantly be both a pain-giver and pain-receiver, and he'd always be walled in. So he prayed to God and asked for His favour to bring exactly the opposite to pass. And God granted his petition—the implication being that he received what he asked for because he was an honourable man.

The men of Jabesh essentially did exactly as Jabez did. They had seen Saul at his best—they had seen him turn the people of Benjamin, *the son of might, the son of the right hand*, from a heritage of perversity to honourable leadership. They too wanted the hand of God to be with them, just as it had been for Saul at the start. They too were honourable men—turning the 'besh', *shame*, within their town's name to its opposite, simply by keeping their word.

Every name encodes both identity and destiny. Within a name God places a high calling and, throughout our lives, He summons us to fulfil the works He has prepared beforehand for us to complete. He has a destiny for us as individuals, but he also has a destiny for our family to achieve. However, although I've used the word 'destiny', there is nothing fated about it all. There is always a choice. We can turn our backs on God's calling—and most people do.

But not the people of Jabesh Gilead. Sure, they were up against the odds with 'besh', *pain* and *shame* in the name of their town. However, *humility* might sometimes be a better word here than *shame*.[70] Humility is essential to honour. When Scripture tells us that *'Jabez was more honourable than his brothers,'* it's letting us know he was a humble man. In choosing humility, in choosing to bypass pride, we choose to position ourselves for God's favour. The people of Jabesh kept their promise, even though some of them might have thought it was made null and void on Saul's death. This wasn't just about honour, it was also about humility.

When we keep our promises, particularly when it's inconvenient, risky or disadvantageous, we allow integrity to ripen in our lives. Our strength of character doesn't mature in times of ease and comfort. It matures when we make tough decisions that go against our own self-interest.

To remove the defilement on us, and on our land, we have to use one specific fruit of the Spirit: shalom, *peace*. But shalom is more than *peace*; it's also integrity, soundness, wholeness, completeness, welfare, prosperity. And there are pre-requisites to shalom: honour, justice, restitution, reconciliation.

That's why David couldn't complete this healing. Not when his capital was Jerusalem, a city in the territory of Benjamin, rather than in his own tribal lands of Judah.

But the Son of David, Jesus the Restorer, could and did complete the work that Saul left unfinished, that David left unfinished, and that even Elijah and John the Baptist left unfinished. He is the incomparable and peerless 'Author and Finisher' of our faith.

Prayer

FATHER IN HEAVEN, ABBA FATHER,

Again I am sorry. Help me to repent for the many times I have compared myself with others. Forgive me for the times I've seen myself as better and harboured secret pride. Forgive me for the times I've been jealous of seeing others cross over into their calling. Forgive me for my anger and belief that they had your favour and I didn't. My greed and my 'Where's mine?' attitude meant I was never quite satisfied with all You did for me. I further dishonoured You by failing to thank You, or even notice the abundance of good things, pressed down and overflowing, that You provided.

I ask Jesus to come with His strength and might to empower my repentance, and to enable me to see, acknowledge and appreciate You. I implore You for a true vision of who You are, what You do and how You want me to respond honourably.

Help me, Jesus, to appreciate who You are and what You have done during Your lifetime as well as by Your death on the Cross. I believe; help my unbelief.

In the name of Jesus of Nazareth, the Author and Finisher of my faith. Amen.

An Egyptian statue depicting Reshef (Resheph) with Egyptian white crown combined with the head of a gazelle. From the collection in the Metropolitan Museum of Art, New York.

3

A Long Awakening

AS I WAS GROWING UP, some activities would make me extremely uncomfortable. Blowing out candles on a birthday cake and making a wish. Dropping a coin in a wishing well. Spotting a shooting star and making a wish. Listening to Disney's Jiminy Cricket sing, *'When you wish upon a star...'* Around me, the 'harmless fun' was accompanied by an internal warning siren sounding an inexplicably loud alarm.[71]

A wish is a corrupted prayer.

Wishcraft is the first step into witchcraft.

On the burning coals of the altar of incense that represent the prayers of the saints, I'd placed a huge lump of malodorous resin that never burned away. It was, as I'd realised even at six years old, bigger than a mountain. It was like an entire range and, on the maps of my soul, it was labelled, 'I want hell to move.' My only real sense of the existence of this spiritual disaster zone was a series of nightmares and an anxiety about wishing.

As Christmas rolled around to Easter the following year, a miracle happened. God stepped in. In the last week before the holiday break, my classroom teacher would begin the day by telling part of the story of the death and resurrection of Jesus. 'He did this for you,' Miss Gaffney said. 'He died for you.'

I looked into my heart and knew she was speaking the truth. So I made up my mind to live for Him. But, looking back and knowing what I do now, every time I prayed—every time I threw a pinch of fragrant incense onto the altar of intercession in my life—the fetid smell of that lump of resin would overwhelm the sweet aroma of prayer. The wish would defile the whole.

Resheph, an officer of God's entourage, can be described—just like Leviathan—by the symbols within the Inner Court:

- the burning coals of the altar of incense
- the bread of the Presence waiting to be consumed by His holy ones
- the flames of the seven-branched menorah

As the burning coals on the altar of incense, Resheph is meant to be the agent of wafting a fine perfume of prayer to God. The piquant scent of victory, of our overcoming through the grace of Jesus, is meant to rise to Him. But if we're loading the altar with our wishes and wants, desires and cravings, instead of prayers aligned with His will, we're lighting the fires of an unholy stench and nonetheless expecting heaven's favour.

Leviathan is going to come back so fast with a smackdown we won't know what hit us or why. Just as it did for King Uzziah.

Resheph's companion as a divine throne guardian is Deber, *pestilence*. However, 'deber' comes from 'dabar', *to speak, declare, preach, pronounce, proclaim, promise, sing, say, state, utter.* When prophecy becomes more about wish-fulfilment than the will of God, we allow Deber entry into our lives. When preaching becomes more about money for empire-building than provision for the journey, we allow Resheph free rein in our lives—even when we're not doing the preaching, but the responding. When the gospel becomes a business rather than a gift, we hand over to Leviathan legal rights that will, sooner or later, come back to bite us.

Human beings are incredibly inventive when it comes to avoiding God and ducking into a false refuge to be safe from His presence. As I've written on false refuges over the years, several people have admitted their surprise to find that *prayer* was their place of consolation away from God. How subtle a diversionary tactic of the enemy is that? Prayer, of all things! Yet, over the last half-century, we've seen all sorts of ways wishes have been dolled up, disguised, and used to warp our prayer life. The once-popular technique of 'name it and claim it' has been revamped over time into variations such as 'declaring and decreeing', 'word of faith' or creating your ideal world through your words. Within the mystic tradition, 'centering prayer' that involves emptying the mind has made a revival as has mantra-facilitated meditation[72] and sacred labyrinths.[73] And there have always been the celebrity-sanctioned intercessions that require exact wording or daily repetition to achieve their desired effect.

Like the little girl with the curl in the middle of her forehead who, when she was good was very, very good and when she was bad, she was horrid—these prayer methods combine a golden kernel of deep truth with the ever-present potential for contamination by heavy-duty occult practices involving wishing, visualisation and transactions such as defective trading or flawed sowing. Intimacy with God has been replaced by potent verbal rituals for achieving particular goals. Back a century ago, a potent verbal ritual would have been recognised for what it really is: the practice of magic.

The hardest thing God asks of us is to give up our power. He gave us the power in the first place but He wants us to surrender it back to Him. He makes massive promises in His Word but, in our desire to see them manifest in the timing we'd prefer, we tend to use the authority He has delegated to us against Him. We want what we want *when* we want it. So we ask for things in prayer that will defame His name, and thus dishonour Him at the 'altar of incense'. Then we wonder why massive retaliation has come our way.

The overarching theme of the previous book in this series is honour, along with Leviathan's legal rights to retaliate against dishonour. As I followed the breadcrumb trail that led inexorably to 'rizpah' and thence to 'resheph', along with all the issues of honour and dishonour associated with those words, I felt uneasy. From the beginning, right from the very first time I realised Resheph was a high-level cosmic power not just a heap of burning coals on an incense altar, I was torn about its identity. Was it—or was it not—Leviathan by another name? Or another 'face'? After all, the cherubim have four faces—ox, man, lion, eagle—so it's not inconceivable that the seraphim also have more than one. On the other hand, was it perhaps more accurately one of the seven 'heads' of Leviathan? What exactly was the relationship between the two?

Towards the end of my research I realised the problem was my mode of thinking. I want to flag this because, if you're like me, you'll continue reading still harbouring preconceived notions you're not even aware you have. I discovered that I still have a fair few vestiges of scientific rationalism holed up in the back of my mind and, secretly, I wanted everything to line up in nice, neat western cultural categories. A crocodile is nothing like a stag, I said to myself. Therefore Resheph and Leviathan can't possibly be the same. Yet they had so much in common, I felt the constant tension of holding tight to this position.

I didn't realise I needed to adopt an eastern mindset until I mentioned to some friends who'd been born in Asia that I was struggling to reconcile Leviathan's connection with honour to Resheph's connection with death. They were completely bemused by my conflict in this regard. Honour and death were, in their view, natural partners. In my framework of logic, I could see nothing in common between honour and death, but they saw them as inseparable.

The fledgling kingdom of Israel was flawed from the start. God told the people not to desire a king, but they insisted. And so began a convoluted and complex epic of defilement and occasional depravity, spanning nearly thirty generations.

Your mind is probably reeling from all of the interwoven stories—Saul, David, Uzziah, Korah, Jonathan the Levite—that I've highlighted up to this point. Yet these represent just a few of the labyrinthine intricacies of layered dishonour in Israel's history. I hope they give you some sense of the devastating mess Jesus faced when He set out to complete the work of honour left unfinished by the warriors of Jabesh Gilead. Although they'd honoured Saul in death, they also brought defilement upon their own territory because of his covenant with Sheol. They may have tried exorcism, given his burial spot under a tamarisk tree but, if they did, we know their efforts didn't quite work.

And we know that because in the time of Elijah, it was ravens—death-eaters—that brought him food. It's astonishing that these unclean birds renowned for ignoring the needs of their own young supplied those of the man of God. Yes, it was a miracle orchestrated by God, partly in provision, partly in prophecy. Prophetic because, while this ravine saw ravens in the time of Elijah, it later saw a descending dove in the time of the Elijah-who-was-to-come. The raven, the death-eater, followed by the dove, the peace-bringer, symbolises a surpassingly great promise: death will be swallowed up in victory and then peace and world-restoration will come.[74]

After the Feast of Hanukkah—the Festival of Lights—Jesus came to Bethany-beyond-the-Jordan to hide from those conspiring to kill him. While there He received a message:

Now a man named Lazarus was sick. He was from Bethany, the village of Mary and her sister Martha. (This Mary, whose brother Lazarus now lay sick, was the same one who poured perfume on the Lord and wiped His feet with her hair.) So the sisters sent word to Jesus, 'Lord, the one You love is sick.'

When He heard this, Jesus said, 'This sickness will not end in death. No, it is for God's glory so that God's Son may be glorified through it.' Now Jesus loved Martha and her sister and Lazarus. So when He heard that Lazarus was sick, He stayed where He was two more days, and then He said to His disciples, 'Let us go back to Judea.'

'But Rabbi,' they said, 'a short while ago the Jews there tried to stone You, and yet You are going back?'

Jesus answered, 'Are there not twelve hours of daylight? Anyone who walks in the daytime will not stumble, for they see by this world's light. It is when a person walks at night that they stumble, for they have no light.'

After He had said this, He went on to tell them, 'Our friend Lazarus has fallen asleep; but I am going there to wake him up.'

His disciples replied, 'Lord, if he sleeps, he will get better.' Jesus had been speaking of his death, but His disciples thought He meant natural sleep.

So then He told them plainly, 'Lazarus is dead, and for your sake I am glad I was not there, so that you may believe. But let us go to him.'

> *Then Thomas (also known as Didymus) said to the rest of the disciples, 'Let us also go, that we may die with Him.'*

> John 11:1-16 NIV

The Resurrection and the Life was about the confront Resheph, the so-called 'lord of the underworld'. In doing so, He was about to heal that weeping wound Saul had inflicted on the kingdom.

Yet He was also working on another historical healing, again involving a fatal threshold, while He was in the hill country of Gilead.

> *Jephthah made a vow to the Lord: 'If you give the Ammonites into my hands, whatever comes out of the door of my house to meet me when I return in triumph from the Ammonites will be the Lord's, and I will sacrifice it as a burnt offering.'*
>
> *Then Jephthah went over to fight the Ammonites, and the Lord gave them into his hands...*
>
> *When Jephthah returned to his home in Mizpah, who should come out to meet him but his daughter, dancing to the sound of timbrels! She was an only child. Except for her he had neither son nor daughter. When he saw her, he tore his clothes and cried, 'Oh no, my daughter! You have brought me down and I am devastated. I have made a vow to the Lord that I cannot break.'*
>
> *'My father,' she replied, 'you have given your word to the Lord. Do to me just as you promised, now that the Lord has avenged you of your enemies, the Ammonites. But grant me this one request,' she*

> *said. 'Give me two months to roam the hills and weep with my friends, because I will never marry.'*
>
> Judges 11:30–37 NIV

Jesus spent around two months with His closest friends in the hills of Gilead, just as Jephthah's daughter did. Was He mourning? Certainly He was expecting soon to die, as the final comment of Thomas indicates.

The meaning of Jephthah is connected to 'miphtan', *threshold*, but this is not an ordinary threshold, it is a defiled one dedicated to the spirit of Python.[75] While Jephthah's daughter remains unnamed in both Scripture and rabbinical commentaries, nonetheless in the first century she was identified, perhaps traditionally, as She'ula—a name that is the feminine form of Sha'ul, Hebrew for Saul.[76] It was also said She'ula was well-named because her bridal bed was indeed the underworld.

The sacrifice of Jephthah's daughter is a foreshadowing of the atoning death of Jesus. But in His re-enactment of her period of mourning, He not only honours her but begins the work of healing the defiled threshold that goes back to the time of Jephthah the Gileadite.

In Arthurian legend, the motif of the wasteland is connected to the maiming of the Fisher King—a sovereign whose land cannot be healed and whose body cannot be healed until the right question is asked about a sacred procession in which the Grail—the Cup of the

Last Supper of Jesus and His disciples—is held aloft. The question isn't a hard one. It's simply: 'What does this mean?'

Noble knights come and go, but no one asks the question. In the meantime, the Fisher King lies in bed or goes fishing in a small boat on the river near his castle. Finally, of course, the right knight comes along, allows his curiosity to overcome his courtesy, and heals the king as well as restores the fertility of the land.

In Arthurian legend, the quest is the heart of the story. The journey across the landscape to right wrongs, rescue damsels in distress, dispatch ogres and dragons—that's the central core of most stories. In modern fantasy, the quest is generally so important a map is essential to follow the hero's route. And in *Dealing with Leviathan*, I briefly indicated the significance of the lines and hubs Leviathan creates in the landscape in order to lay its claim and name on various nations.

There are many myths of heroes who walk the path of the dead but we don't often think of Jesus as doing something similar. But the story of Lazarus, beginning as it does in Bethany-beyond-the-Jordan, shows Jesus traversing the same route as the first king did in death. Like the story of the Fisher King, this is about healing the land. In addition, it has echoes of the myth of Orpheus heading into the underworld to retrieve Eurydice, but with a happy ending!

Jesus had a greater agenda in going to Bethany than just raising his friend Lazarus back to life. He also wanted to heal the kingdom and the very nature of kingship in the process.

Some time previously, Jesus '*had to go through Samaria*' to meet a woman by a well. Not simply for her sake but in order to reunify the ancient kingdoms of Judah and Israel. David's kingdom had split just after the ceremony for his grandson's coronation. Rehoboam had invoked Leviathan. Responding to those who asked for relief from the heavy tax and work burden of Solomon, he arrogantly retorted:

> *Whereas my father burdened you with a heavy yoke, I will add to your yoke. Whereas my father scourged you with whips, I will scourge you with scorpions.*
>
> 1 Kings 12:11 BSB

Leviathan's symbols include the scorpion. So his words not only called on Leviathan, he did so at a place where Resheph had a shrine.[77] As a consequence Rehoboam received the usual reward for pride: a fall. The backlash that came his way was, like that which befell Uzziah, Jeroboam and Korah, unusually swift. His kingdom was torn asunder.

It was never restored until Jesus, waiting by a well in Samaria—at the same place Rehoboam lost the kingdom—asked a woman for a drink. In God's economy there was a great deal more going on in this incident than the reunification of the Kingdom of David. Yet one thing Jesus did not do there was lift the defilement from Saul's covenant with Sheol. To accomplish that, He retraced the same route Saul's bones were carried after they were disinterred at Jabesh Gilead and then re-buried in the tomb of Kish at Zela.

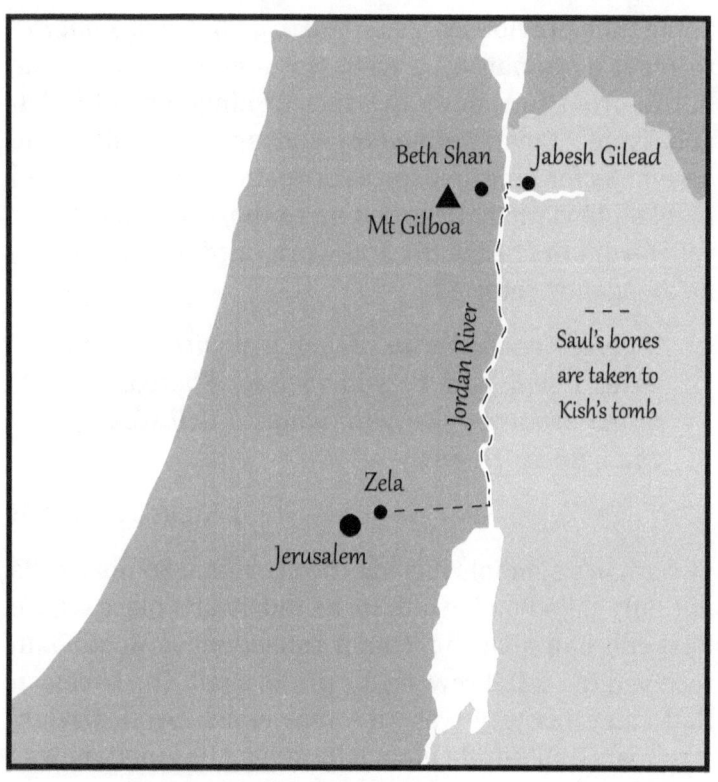

The pattern, showing that His journey has numinous overtones of God walking the path of the dead and travelling that same trail of past pain, lurks just below the surface and is made accessible to us through the clues given via the placenames.

Jesus started at Bethany-beyond-the-Jordan and travelled to Bethany. That congruence of names isn't coincidental and it isn't the only pair either. Bethany-beyond-the-Jordan was in the vicinity of the ancient town of Jabesh Gilead. Bethany on the other hand was in the vicinity of Jerusalem which, in ancient times, was known as Jebus.

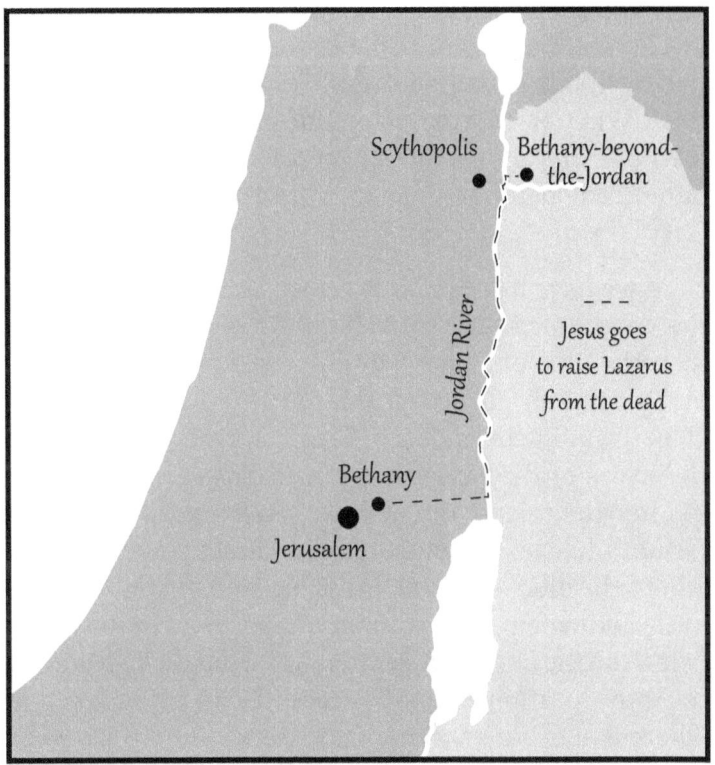

Jabesh and Jebus are basically the same word (hence, no doubt, why Jabesh got designated Gilead, in order to distinguish it with a regional tag). Both names have connotations of *pain*, *persecution* and *walled up*. This makes Jabesh and Jebus a fitting match for Bethany which, according to Jerome in the second century, means *house of affliction*. Now Jerome's interpretation is widely disputed by scholars but I'm going to accept it because it slots neatly into the pattern on two counts. First, *affliction* makes it cognate with Jabesh and Jebus, and secondly, *affliction* suggests the original spelling was Beth-oni. This is a clear pointer to Benjamin.

The village of Bethany was not only situated in the territory of the clan of Benjamin—as Jerusalem was—it may well have been named after the progenitor of the tribe. When Rachel lay dying, she called her second son 'Ben-oni', *son of my sorrow* or *son of my affliction.* His father renamed him 'Benjamin', *son of my right hand* or *son of the south.*

Here we have a clue that Jesus was walking the path of the dead much further back into the heart of tragedy than the time of Saul's tainting of the kingship. He was also setting in place a healing for the heartbreak that came from Rachel's death. This is further hinted at by the name of the place in the wilderness He withdrew to after the raising of Lazarus: it was Ephraim, named for both Rachel's grandson and indirectly for the place where she died. Although Jacob buried her at Ephrathah near Bethlehem, by the time of Saul her tomb was at Zelzah on the border of Benjamin and Judah. This may be the same location as Zela[78] where Kish had his tomb and where Saul's bones, along with those of his sons, were finally laid to rest. However scholars have identified Zelzah as Beit Jala, about six kilometres from Jerusalem while Zela has been identified as Khirbet Salah,[79] about three kilometres from Jerusalem.

Now John gave the distance from Bethany[80] to Jerusalem about fifteen stadia—making it also, like Zela, three kilometres away. So: was Bethany the ancient site of Kish's tomb at Zela? It would be an exquisitely lovely touch if it were so. The repair work of Jesus would then be tailored so neatly to rebuild the ancient ruins so they could show forth the glory they were always meant to do. Much as I'd like to be able to identify Zela and Bethany as the same place, the weight of archaeology—at least at present—is against it.

This epic of trauma and restoration spans millennia. From start-to-finish, it's about honour and dishonour, so it's therefore not a coincidence that, when Jesus spoke about honour, it was in the vicinity of Jabesh. We can learn from those ancient people of Gilead who, having gained an understanding of honour, never forgot it.

> *Jesus said, 'This sickness will not end in death. No, it is for God's glory so that God's Son may be glorified through it.'*

John 11:4 NIV

He was speaking about Lazarus, having just received a message he was gravely ill. Once He'd left Bethany-beyond-the-Jordan for Bethany and there He approached the tomb of Lazarus, He said to Martha:

> *'Did I not tell you that if you believe, you will see the glory of God?'*

John 11:40 NIV

Jesus was making a new point about honour. Perhaps His words are elusive, but remember that *glory* and *honour* are identical in Hebrew: 'kabod'.

He said:

> *'This sickness will not end in death. No, it is for God's **glory** so that God's Son may be **glorified** through it.'*

However, to the Hebrew mind, that was also:

> *'This sickness will not end in death. No, it is for God's **honour** so that God's Son may be **honoured** through it.'*

Jesus went across the Jordan and travelled to the place where the bones of the first king of a united Israel were finally interred in honour. But He went to show death is not the end. He went to raise the dead, He went not only to display honour to God but also God's honour towards us. Did He go, as the Son of David, to honour Saul's memory? I think He did.

Belatedly, David himself had honoured Saul but there's one small detail I think suggests Jesus had Saul in mind far more than David when it came to the kingship. This detail is, again, about location. It was not in Bethlehem that Jesus was anointed king—as David had been, or even Hebron or Jerusalem his later capitals. Nor was Jesus anointed at the Gihon Spring, as Solomon had been.

Instead He was anointed at Bethany. Mary anointed and washed Him with the living water of her tears on the evening before He rode a donkey into Jerusalem and the people hailed Him with cries of: 'Hosanna to the Son of David!'

Riding a donkey was a symbol honouring another son of David, Solomon, going to his coronation; however, the anointing at Bethany honoured the House of Saul.

Still, let us turn our minds back to Lazarus and to what happened there. Lazarus, as previously indicated, was a form of Eleazar, which has the same meaning as Azariah. Note the identical elements: **Lazar**us | *El*e**azar** | **Azar**i*ah*. Now Azariah was another name for Uzziah, the king who was stricken with leprosy when he tried to make an offering at the incense altar during the time of Isaiah.

Eleazar, Lazarus, Azariah all mean *God has helped* or *God is my support*. Uzziah on the other hand means *God is my strength*. There's not too much difference on the surface between *God is my support* and *God is my strength*, and thus these names are highly suggestive of a name covenant between God and Uzziah. If this is the case, it goes a long way towards explaining why Uzziah got such a swift smackdown when he began to perform the duties reserved for a priest.

A name covenant and the threshold covenant associated with it entail extra responsibility in terms of faithfulness to God. The new level of intimacy that comes with a name covenant[81] makes treachery possible in a way previously unattainable.

There are so many Scriptural examples that should have warned Uzziah of the spiritual peril he was flirting with—which include not only that of Saul but also of his near namesake Uzzah.

David was setting up his capital in Jerusalem when he decided to bring the Ark of the Covenant up from Kiriath-Jearim:

> *They set the ark of God on a new cart and brought it from the house of Abinadab, which was on the hill. Uzzah and Ahio, the sons of Abinadab, were guiding the new cart... When they came to the threshing floor of Nacon, Uzzah reached out and took hold of the ark of God, because the oxen had stumbled. And the anger of the Lord burned*

> *against Uzzah, and God struck him down on the spot for his irreverence, and he died there beside the ark of God.*
>
> 2 Samuel 6:3–7 BSB

Uzzah means *strength*, Uzziah means *God is my strength*. At some point, King Uzziah lost sight of the *God-is* part of his name and chose to trust in himself and no one else. Scripture is littered with disasters that we've brought on ourselves and our descendants when we've felt God has failed to keep His promise to us. Four thousand years later, the consequences of Sarai's plan to help God overcome her barrenness and give Abram a son are still outworking themselves in a cauldron of mutual dishonour and hatred in the Middle East.

God makes incredible pledges of peace and prosperity to us like this one:

> *'If you follow My statutes and carefully observe My commandments, I will give you rains in their season, and the land will yield its produce... you will have your fill of food to eat and will dwell securely in your land.'*
>
> Leviticus 26:3–5 BSB

That's about as clear-cut as it gets: God promises to look after us, conditional only on the fact we obey Him. David testifies to God's providence:

> *I was young and now I am old, yet I have never seen the righteous forsaken or their children begging bread.*
>
> Psalm 37:25 NIV

That too looks like a promise. Technically, it's an observation. David is making the comment that, over his lifetime, he's seen God's faithfulness time and time again. However, the psalm confirms some very definite promises spoken directly by God. But know what I think about Psalm 37:25? And Leviticus—not to mention Exodus and Deuteronomy and countless others—with all their promises? It's this: David must have lived in a bubble.

Because I've seen believers, with all the imputed righteousness of Christ, begging plenty of times. I've seen them follow the clear guidance of God and lose everything in the process. This is particularly true when they are attempting to cross over the threshold into their calling. They get squeezed by Python, whacked by Leviathan, abused by Belial, wasted by Rachab, skewered by Lilith.

Now most people, when this happens, get mired in a quicksand of Scripture mixed with theology. Theology tells us we're righteous in Christ. That messes with our concepts of grace, giving most of us the impression that, since perfect obedience is an impossibility, we can dispense with any obedience at all. We don't realise that grace is the gift to make the impossible possible—to empower us to walk in obedience even when that's the last thing we feel like doing.

God's conditions haven't changed. When a meltdown has happened on the threshold, we need to step aside, talk to Him and ask, 'Where did I turn aside to my own strength? When did I become like Uzzah and, with good intentions but in total ignorance of danger, try to right the situation? When was I like Uzziah, taking things into my own hands because my situation needed urgent attention and I felt I had to go to the altar because Jesus, my High Priest, wasn't handling things the "right" way? How do I get back from where I am to where You want me to be?'

God's promises are true. But when they are apparently going down the tubes, it isn't the time to stand on them more fervently, or declare them more loudly or repeat them more often. It's time to turn to Him and have a heart-to-heart about why things are not working out. Is it about disobedience or is it because there are matters of honour at stake?

When Jesus was first informed about Lazarus, He waited two days before doing anything. Now it's not uncommon to hear that Jesus wanted to be sure Lazarus was definitely dead by the time He got there. But I have other suspicions, based on the strange statement He made in response to the disciples' protests about the risks of returning to Judea:

> *'Are there not twelve hours of daylight? Anyone who walks in the daytime will not stumble, for they see by this world's light. It is when a person walks at night that they stumble, for they have no light.'*

In the Greek, the first question could be alternatively rendered: *Are there not twelve periods in a year?* And the last phrase more accurately says: *'the light is not in them.'* When expressed like this, it seems possible Jesus is making a covenant statement in relation to light and the seasons. He went into hiding just after Hanukkah—the Feast of Dedication, the Festival of Lights. Was He waiting to come out of hiding until the winter season, the time of darkness and the dead, was over? How would that be marked?

Possibly by Purim, a celebration renowned in our era for mask-wearing—thus subtly referring to Esther, the orphaned Hebrew girl who became the Queen of Persia. The name 'Esther' derives from Ishtar, a goddess associated with the planet Venus. And although 'Esther' means *star* in Persian, in the Hebrew language it sounds like 'astir', meaning *hiddenness* or *concealment*.[82] This is appropriate to the story of Esther—the only book of Scripture in which the name of God is not apparent. In addition, it's appropriate to Esther's life and her masked identity as a Jew. Her real name was Hadassah, and she was another risk-taking daughter of the tribe of Benjamin.[83]

The story of Esther is prophetic of the hidden, unrecognised Saviour, 'the Morning Star'. This is a title of Jesus given in Revelation 22:16. Esther's name refers to the planet Venus, the 'morning star' which is also the 'evening star'.

When Venus transitions from being the evening star to the morning star, it's hidden from sight for three days. The three-day fast of Esther[84] may well reflect this aspect of her name. At the end of this period of fasting, Esther went to the king to plead for her people. Such an action is prophetic of Jesus' ascent to the Father after His three days, hidden in the tomb. He said to Mary Magdalene in the garden:

> *'Do not touch Me, for not yet have I ascended to the Father. Now go to My brothers and say to them, "I am ascending to My Father and your Father, and to My God and your God."'*
>
> John 20:17 BLB

At first sight, it seems like a bit of overkill in identifying which God He's talking about but I've come to see specificity as very wise. We can't be too sure what hidden covenants lurk in our family line.

So why does Jesus delay for two days at Bethany-beyond-the-Jordan? I suspect that He wanted to come out of hiding on the third day—foreshadowing His rising from the tomb but also looking back to Esther and her confrontation with Haman, a descendant of Agag.[85] Saul had been commanded by God to execute this Amalekite king but he'd spared his life while he set about installing a monument in his own honour. It was left to Samuel to slay Agag.

This was *the* critical incident—dishonour of God and honour of self—that caused God to reject Saul as king. Before that, he'd been rebuked and told he would not be able to establish a dynasty but that was the moment when God turned against him.

Death and honour were entwined together—and not just for Saul. Also for Esther as she chose to risk her life and appear before the king without being summoned. It might appear that Esther managed to escape the general tendency in the tribe of Benjamin to name their children for aspects of the underworld. But no. The most famous story of her namesake is *Ishtar's Descent,* in which the goddess of love, storms and war attempts to conquer the domain of her sister, the Queen of the Underworld. Ishtar is judged guilty of extreme arrogance, struck dead, but then allowed to return to life after three days. However, her husband is forced to replace her in the underworld—but allowed out for six months each year. His return marks the beginning of the spring season.

Jesus had already confronted Ishtar's husband, Dumuzid, in his guise as Tammuz, *'the Bread Come Down from Heaven'* during the miraculous feeding of the five thousand. But in His actions leading up to the raising of Lazarus, He showed that His war against the realm of death encompassed far more than just Resheph.

Ishtar, too, and her sister Erishkigal would not stand against His 'herem', His war of total annihilation. Death would die. And none of this substitute business would be permitted. No one's life was going to have to be traded so Lazarus could return. It was going to be a gift of grace and love. Just as His own resurrection would be.

No sooner had Jesus defeated one spiritual opponent than another took its place. His words to His disciples, *'Anyone who walks in the daytime will not stumble, for they see by this world's light. It is when a person walks at night that they stumble, for they have no light'* with the repeated reference to *stumbling* and *not having light within* suggests He is speaking of covenant. Throughout the Law and the Prophets, *stumbling* refers to refusing threshold covenant—that is, rejecting God's invitation to hospitality and His call to join with Him and partake of the delights of His banqueting table. So who would this covenant be with, if not with Yahweh? The words of Jesus don't immediately suggest Ishtar.

The contrast of day and night, along with the repeated reference to light, suggests the Hebrew words, 'shemesh', *daylight* and 'layil', *night*. In turn these suggest Shamash, the 'lord of the sun', and Lilith, the 'queen of the night'.

Shamash was a Canaanite godling repeatedly equated with the Mesopotamian deity, Nergal, who was associated with death, war and destruction. Since 'sun' and 'death' don't seem immediately and obviously linked, the godling Shamash is suggested by some commentators to be the killing heat of noonday. Nergal is associated with the high heat of the summer solstice as well as the midday sun. Saul's grandfather, Ner, may have been named for Nergal—keeping the death theme in the family naming going quite nicely, since Nergal was the husband of Erishkigal, the Queen of the Underworld. Ner is generally listed as *a lamp*, but more strictly its meaning is *a burner*.[86]

Does this sound like Resheph? It should! I haven't been able to find any scholars who *directly* connect Resheph and Shamash, but many equate Shamash with Nergal, and Nergal with Resheph.

Jesus was referring these underworld deities in a way that's very allusive by modern Western standards.[87] But we truly have to put aside the expectation that His speech will be as direct as we want for our era, and not as inscrutable as the Middle Eastern culture of His own day. He spoke in parables that even those closest to Him were baffled by. He made the point in Luke 8:10 that He didn't explain Himself because it was not for everyone to understand His teaching. Even when He told His disciples Lazarus had died, it wasn't particularly clear:

> *'Our friend Lazarus has fallen asleep; but I am going there to wake him up.'*

Perhaps one of the reasons Jesus was so indirect in speech is because He encoded the weight of history in His words. One of the Hebrew words for *sleep* is 'shenah', a word that should remind us of Beth Shan, the place where the Philistines exposed the bodies of Saul and his sons on the fortress walls before they were taken to Jabesh. (In later times, the spelling of Beth Shan changed very slightly and it became Beit She'an, *house of rest, repose* or *peace*. Here I'm focusing on the original spelling which, besides *sleep*, also suggests *year* or *change*.)[88]

In addition, there is a Hebrew word that suggests more than *being woken*, but actually *being awoken from the sleep of death*. It is 'quts' and it's derived from 'qayits', *summer fruit* or *ripe fruit*. Amos has a vision of a basket of ripe fruit and is told that the meaning is that the time is ripe for retribution to fall on the land.[89] Jesus is turning this concept around: the time is ripe in His calendar for revivification. And so He went from Bethany-beyond-the-Jordan to Bethany, with every step breaking the power of Saul's ancient covenant with the underworld.

Covenants are forever. They don't have an end-date—they don't suddenly cease to exist on the deaths of those who raised the covenant in the first place. They don't expire after three or four generations. Instead they follow family lines for as long as the family remains. The covenant God made with Abram about four millennia ago still applies to his descendants today. Yet, there is a vitally important exception to this rule:

> *Your covenant with death will be annulled, and your agreement with Sheol will not stand.*
>
> Isaiah 28:18 ESV

God specifically excludes a covenant with Death or with Sheol from the general rule that such pacts are everlasting. In fact, as Isaiah proclaims, God says He will cancel them. This is exactly what Jesus went to Bethany to do: to annul a covenant with the monarchs of the underworld. No, actually, 'annul' isn't quite the right word. *Annihilate* is more like it.

When Jesus arrived at Bethany six days after He first received the news about Lazarus, He was first approached by Martha. Then He saw Mary weeping and the people around her wailing and:

> *...a deep anger welled up within Him, and He was deeply troubled.*
>
> John 11:33 NLT

A deep anger: in Greek, this is related to the *snorting of a warhorse*. No prizes for guessing that Resheph was associated with war and warhorses.

In raising Lazarus, Jesus tore down the gates of the underworld to confront Resheph. Although there's much more to explore in this episode, let's sideline it until we look at the Resurrection itself. The time is ripe to examine some practical implications of what Jesus did.

Prayer

It is vitally important to recognise that prayer is about relationship with the Father. None of the prayers in this book are intended as a formula but as a guideline to help you realign yourself with the holy Trinity. They are meant as a starting point for a conversation.

Transformation is only possible as you hold onto the hem of Jesus' prayer shawl and ask Him to mediate before the Father for you. In the end, it's all about Him!

WOE IS ME! I HAVE UNCLEAN LIPS and I live amongst a people of unclean lips. I have dishonoured You, Abba, first of all. I have dishonoured my leaders in government, employment, church, family. I don't even know what true honour looks like. My thoughts are tainted by cultural and ancestral corruption. I want to give You honour and glory but my idea of it is so shabby, I don't have a clue where to start to rectify the problem.

Forgive me for my sins of thought, word, action and inaction. I have sinned in what I have thought about others and situations; also in what I have said about others and situations; in both how I have acted and failed to act.

Heavenly Father, I have also sinned by my silence. Forgive me for the times when the proposed laws and regulations of this nation were not in accord with Your word and I said and did nothing. My silence was as dishonouring and disrespectful of You as my words and actions were. I kept silent because I did not want to be branded a bigot or a hater. I didn't want to dishonour others and so I chose to dishonour You. Abba, help me to honour You in all I think, say and do. I repent of not being true to You and so not being true to myself. Convict me at a heart level that when others call me a bigot and a hater they are saying more about themselves than they are about me.

I truly repent, Abba. Jesus, loving Mediator, please empower the words I have spoken.

> Father in heaven, I give You today
> All that I think and do and say,
> And I unite it with all that was done,
> By Jesus Christ Your only Son. Amen.

4
Paths of the Dead

MY MOTHER ONCE HAD an enigmatic vision. It happened during the worship time at a church she was visiting in another state. She was helping my dad facilitate a prayer ministry seminar in a bayside city there. The worship leader was a gifted musician who had converted from a Muslim background. Twenty minutes into the singing on the fourth day, a 'screen' in my mum's mind switched on suddenly. To her surprise, she 'saw' a young woman running through the lush grass of a lovely green field. The mystery woman was dressed in a sheer, shimmery white dress and her long, fair hair floated on the breeze. With her was a young boy aged about eight. He was holding her hand and was wearing a crisply ironed white shirt with black pants held up by braces. On his feet were a pair of sturdy sandals. It was a delightful, old-fashioned scene—the happiest of happy pictures.

She immediately asked in her mind: 'What on earth is that?' The answer came back instantly: 'Teresa Joy and Emrys.'

She almost fainted and had to sit down very quickly. Because Teresa Joy and Emrys were her grandchildren—my sister's children. Emrys had been stillborn eight years previously, and Teresa Joy had been born eleven years before him. She had had genetic abnormalities that caused her premature death as a very young child.

My dad realised something was wrong as soon as my mum sat down abruptly. However, she had been stirred up into such a serious emotional mess that she couldn't say anything about her experience until much later in the day. Then, after talking with him and two other team members, she felt she was meant to share the vision with the entire group. So the next morning, just after the worship concluded, she did just that. As she was speaking, there was a sudden thud behind her. The worship leader had collapsed to the floor in a faint.

People rushed forward to help revive him. And then his story emerged. It transpired that he had had two sons with exactly the same syndrome as Teresa Joy. They also had died very young. His deep, unrevealable belief was that, because he had been a Muslim at the time, he would never see them again—even in the next life. It was an unspeakable grief to him but my mother's recounting of her vision gave him hope.

For my mum, the vision ultimately raised so many questions. She is aware it was given to her to heal the wounded heart of this musician. However, it had never entered her head previously that, after children die, they continue to mature. She still has some issues with that. But she is also aware that God would not give anyone false hope, just for the sake of hope itself. He is the Way, the Truth and the Life, as well as the Resurrection and the Life.

As I reflected on the 'healing of history' that Jesus accomplished through His journey from Bethany-on-the-Jordan to Bethany, I was troubled. I'm a passionate proponent of 'healing history'—that incredibly Jewish concept of 'tikkun olam', *mending the world*. I love to encourage people to follow Jesus into similar endeavours. In fact, that's one of several aspects behind the series, *Jesus and the Healing of History*. It's to say to believers, 'Go out and do likewise! Go and heal history! How hard is it, after all, to ask for a drink of water?' Because that's all it took for Jesus to start the healing of a vicious centuries-old rift between the Samaritans and Jews.

But it wasn't a random question He asked: it was perfectly tailored to the original harm and perfectly targeted at the same kind of person most wounded by past events. Jesus didn't ever say that Nehemiah the cupbearer and Ezra the priest were wrong to force the Israelite men to divorce their foreign wives and abandon the children born of such unions. But His actions speak loudly into the silence. He just asked a woman who'd been through several marriages and had been widowed, sent away or abandoned several times to be His cupbearer.

All the King needs to do to appoint a cupbearer is to ask someone to give Him a drink! He honoured her with the same position as the man who had dishonoured all her people. Still, He didn't make a big deal of it; He made it simple and natural—almost, but not quite routine.

When it comes to healing history, Jesus gives us repeated examples that are neither miraculous nor heroic. They are ordinary events made extraordinary. However He also gives us examples of tough things. Marvellous things. Like, umm, raising the dead. Never having done such myself, it would be tempting to say such healings are for others of greater faith or different gifts or more intense prayer life or... well, any excuse I can think of to let myself off the hook.

But as I contemplated the thought that Jesus has no intention of letting any of us off the hook, I wondered how 'walking the paths of the dead' could be fulfilled in a different way that would bring healing to the land. Immediately I thought of a couple of friends who do so on quite a regular basis. When I suggested this to Irenie and her husband, they were initially startled to think their experiences might qualify as encounters with the underworld. But then it dawned on them that their prayer journeys did indeed follow paths that, in ancient legend, were trackways of the spirits of the dead.

Before we go further, a few brief words on the excessively controversial concept of spirits of the human dead. The Bible treats ghosts, phantoms, wraiths and spectres—at least when these words describe 'spirits of the human dead'—as real. Michael Heiser comments that God forbids us to inquire of the human dead.

> *When you enter the land which the Lord your God gives you, you shall not learn to imitate the detestable things of those nations. There shall not be found among you anyone who makes his son or his daughter pass through the fire, one who uses divination, one who practices witchcraft, or one who interprets omens, or a sorcerer, or one who casts a spell, or a medium, or a spiritist, or one who calls up the dead.*
>
> Deuteronomy 18:9–11 NASB

However, he points out that there is a clear distinction between the prohibitions in this section and elsewhere. He notes that the punishment for contacting *demonic* spirits is death by stoning:

> *A man or woman who is a medium or spiritist among you must be put to death. You are to stone them; their blood will be on their own heads.*
>
> Leviticus 20:27 NIV

However, Heiser also indicates careful reading of both passages shows that this penalty refers specifically to those mediums who contact the *non-human* dead. The same extreme punishment does not apply for contacting the *human* dead.[90]

Nevertheless the *total ban* on consultation still applies. And, if we ignore it, then we have an example of the consequences that follow in the story of Saul. Having eliminated all the mediums in the land, Saul visited the Witch of Endor so the spirit of Samuel could be called up in order to ask his advice about the upcoming battle. It is one thing to inquire of the human dead; it is entirely another to encounter them unintentionally and unexpectedly—as many people have done, for example, in venturing to Culloden Moor.[91]

My personal belief is that it's unwise to be too dogmatic in extending the sanction against *inquiring* of the human dead to an all-encompassing ban. After all, Jesus spoke to Moses at His Transfiguration and who was he at that point, other than a spirit of the human dead? This is not to suggest anyone should ever seek such spirits out; simply that, if they do appear wihtout an invitation, it's wisdom to ask God what's appropriate. Ask Him if He has a purpose in allowing the revelation, similar to my mother's vision of Teresa Joy and Emrys.

The remainder of this chapter distils the story of a healing work Irenie and her husband didn't seek but, as they simply began hiking in obedience to the Lord, mysteriously dropped into their laps.

It is a joy to share with you a little of the walk the Lord has led my husband and me on over the past few years. He has shown us a 'world that is more real than the physical one we live in.' As we have gone on, he has added others to our 'team' and we have continued to learn together. Before I tell of some of our unexpected adventures, I want to emphasise the guidelines we've learned along the way.

[1] First and foremost, *know* Jesus. Know not only who He is—Jesus of Nazareth, King of the Jews, the Great I AM, Lord of all lords, King of all kings, the Great High Priest, the Lamb of God, the One Pure Perfect Sacrifice for the sin of the world, the Lion of the Tribe of Judah, Mighty Conqueror, the Rider on the White Horse, the Prince of Peace, Almighty God, the Name which is above every name, the 'no other name under heaven by which man can be saved', the Prince of Peace, the One who comes and kneels down and washes your feet and kisses your cheeks when you are tired and troubled, the One who tells you not to 'let your heart be troubled but

to trust in God and to trust also in Him', the one who is the Way, the Truth and the Life, the Good Shepherd who knows every one of His sheep—you amongst them—and leads His flock out and calls each one by name—but *know* He is so much more and that a whole book could not cover all of who He is!

Yet knowing who He is, knowing *about* Him, isn't enough. We must know Him personally and intimately, and know His voice. We must also listen to Him and talk with Him regularly.

When I was talking to Him about writing this chapter, He said to me, 'Hear My voice, listen to My voice, know My voice. Be prepared in season and out of season, do not be unprepared. Your preparation is your relationship with Me. Listen to My voice.'

He went on the say, 'Relationship, relationship, it is all about your relationship with Me.'

As Anne has revealed in several books: the kiss of God is the Armour of God! I had seen long ago that every part of the Armour Paul speaks of in Ephesians 6 was another aspect of who Jesus is. So 'the kiss of God' and the close relationship it implies with Jesus is perfectly understandable as divine Armour.

[2] Know that the Lord has called you to the ministry of healing. Do not move on a 'good idea'—wait until it's clear that it is a 'God idea', confirmed by the testimony of independent witnesses. Wait for His perfect timing to move. We (and others

too!) have learned the hard way to ask God before we move on a 'good idea'. He knows if it is truly good or not! We leave ourselves open to attack from the enemy if we go 'on our own'.

[3] Do not rush off to do something God has given you a revelation on. Wait for His timing. So often there is more information you need to know before you go, either for your safety or for the successful completion of the assignment. His timing is perfect—be ready... but wait for His timing. It is incredibly important to be under good sound Spiritual Leadership who you can talk with and who will give you wise counsel.

[4] Do not talk freely to everyone you meet about the revelation God has given you. Don't advertise where He wants you to go or what He wants you to do. Don't splash your mission over social media. These types of assignments are always strategic and, if you hand over God's plans to the enemy because you cannot be trusted to keep His counsel, it will be the last mission you'll receive. Discuss the revelation with Him and only those who are called to 'walk with you', whether they are to accompany you and pray along with you, or to be your outside intercessors, upholding your assignment for success. You need to be covered with prayer by wise intercessors who believe in what you are doing. I usually text or call those who cover us in prayer and just say, 'Please pray for us. We are going walking with the Lion of Judah.' I don't usually have to tell them any more than that.

They just acknowledge my text and I know they are on board with us.

[5] The Lord tells us to sing as we go. Worship is powerful warfare. He often 'gives' us the song to sing as we go—it just 'pops into our minds'. It is about worshipping as we walk. I heard somewhere, and I really liked the idea, that as we sing praises to God, the angels come to sing with us, and that puts 'static' on the enemies' communication lines so our adversaries cannot communicate with each other regarding our presence and mission! Isn't that great? When we walk with my sister, she becomes the 'leader of the singers' and keeps us going! She can sing on very steep hills, long after my puff has gone and my song has disappeared into background worship in my head! If the 'mission' we are on is prayer at home, we always have worship music playing quietly in the background.

[6] In John 5:19 NLT, Jesus said, '*I tell you the truth, the Son can do nothing by Himself. He does only what He sees the Father doing. Whatever the Father does, the Son also does.*' If you are a seer—one who has open visions—what are you seeing? If you are a sensor—one who has a feel for the spiritual environment—what are you touching around about you? If you are a sniffer—one with discernment for the 'smell' of things—what are you detecting? If you are a listener—one who receives words from God—what are you hearing?

Where is Jesus in that 'picture', the 'sensation', the 'aroma', the 'sound' or even the 'taste' you are experiencing? What is He doing? Ask the Lord: 'What is happening here? What do You want me to do?'

Remember, this is *His* mission! You are not alone, you are just privileged to be taken along on this assignment with Him. So, what is your role in this scene? We have found there are spiritual 'critters' we can bind and the Lord deals with them and then the angels remove them. There are others we cannot bind and we ask the Lord to rebuke them. (See Jude 1:9 and 2 Peter 2:11) If you are walking with the Lord on His mission, you never have to fear anything. Just deal with what you see. We have faced many potentially frightening situations with confidence and never been afraid, because the Lion of Judah is at our side!

[7] Unless the Lord specifically asks you, and you are sure it is His voice leading you, never go alone. Remember Jesus sent His disciples out two by two. Ecclesiastes 4:9–12 NIV gives us the picture as to why this is so important,

> *'Two are better than one, because they have a good return for their work: If one falls down, his friend can help him up. But pity the man who falls and has no-one to help him up! Also, if two lie down together, they will keep warm. But how can one keep warm alone? Though one may be overpowered, two can defend themselves. A cord of three strands is not quickly broken.'*

This Scripture has literally played out in our lives on one very eventful mission that was interrupted by falling snow. The vitally important thing is in verse 12b: *'a cord of three strands is not quickly broken.'* This refers to Jesus and whoever else you are working with. Stay close together—in clear view and within easy speaking distance of one other. The enemy is always ready to pick off the tired and the weak! Stay together. Watch each others' backs! The enemy is always the enemy. He doesn't pop up and say with a smile, 'Oh, good afternoon! I am your enemy. I am going to try and take you out.' But that is his mission—to knock you out so you cannot take back what he has stolen. He is guarding his ill-gotten gains and you are in a real battle. Know your enemy! He comes in many guises. 2 Corinthians 11:14 AMP tells us: *'Satan himself masquerades as an angel of light.'*

Your team can be any number greater than one. However, everyone must realise they are walking with the Lord and that He is in charge of the team. We follow Him! All of the team need to be 'on the same page'. They need to be team-players, not lone-rangers.

[8] There is a strong place for fasting when you know you are about to face the enemy. Ask the Lord for His plan. Do not fast on the day you are going on long walks to do any of this ministry. Fast prior to going, if the Lord directs. You cannot do hard physical exercise and fast from food at the same time.

[9] Lastly, in this checklist, let me point out that there are many, many, many layers of defiling history criss-crossing the land. God draws many people from around the world to work quietly at different times to bring different aspects of healing to the land. Occasionally we've met up with His followers who have been called to do 'weird stuff' that's different from the 'weird stuff' we're doing. Does this mean we haven't succeeded in the mission Jesus has taken us on? Does it mean that one way is better than another? No! Some long-standing enemy strongholds take a lot of removing. Think about the effort it takes to bring down a giant tree and then to remove all its roots. You need more than one tool to do that. It's also important to remember that Jesus is not boring, He's creative! He does not do the same things the same way over and over. He knows too well that we would just make that way into a 'method' and then go and do our own thing without Him. It would become a dangerous religious activity!

As Aslan told Lucy in CS Lewis' story, *Prince Caspian*, when she asked him why hadn't appeared to them as he had done the last time they'd seen him, 'I don't do the same thing twice.' Said, of course, with a serious 'twinkle' in his eye!

He is a God of such variety! He doesn't serve up stale, dry or mouldy bread!

Irenie continues:

A few years ago, we were driving past a mountain range when the Lord drew my attention to it. I looked at the peaks with fond memories of having climbed them many, many years previously. My heart warmed as my gaze ranged over the hills, joy flooding my heart as the countryside opened up ahead. What a beautiful landscape!

Two months later I was talking with the Lord about many things, when He just asked what I could see. Now, of course, that's just the sort of thing He asked Jeremiah and Amos and Zechariah, but that fact escaped my notice for quite some time. I just sat quietly for a moment, then I 'saw' this same range of hills that had caught my eye when we'd been driving by. 'Really?' I said. 'Do You really want us to go there?!'

These were BIG hills. The last time we'd climbed them was twenty-four years previously when our children had been teenagers. I realised that the Lord was widening our vision and direction for what He was calling us to do.

It wasn't until eight months later that everything fell into place so we could go. God knows the best time and conditions to send us in. It had taken some time to work out the best way to deal with this mission. We'd had many conversations with the Lord and with each other over it. Remember He knows what we are capable of and will never send us where we are not physically able to go safely. But we still have to trust Him through it all. We have to keep our eyes fixed on Jesus! He is not lost, but we can 'get lost' if we are not staying in close contact with Him.

Our ministry began deep in the middle of this mountainous range—way down by the confluence of two streams. Confluences can be very significant places that need healing. We had been blessed to be helicoptered in, right down onto the spot, near a cabin that could be used for shelter if need be. The Lion of Judah was with us, I had 'seen' Him in the helicopter as we had taken off. As soon as we landed, I could feel the presence of 'trapped spirits' and I knew they were of the ancient people of the land.

The first time we had ever encountered a trapped spirit—or earthbound spirit—we didn't have any idea what was going on. If you'd asked us, we'd have said such a situation was impossible. So we thought this particular spirit was a demonic familiar and we had tried to cast her out. But it turned out she was a trapped human spirit—one who had met with an accident or disease that had taken her life before the number of days allotted to her by the Lord.

We have authority to cast out the demonic, but not human spirits. The realisation this spirit was human and was trapped, 'earthbound', screwed up our theology terribly at the start. We didn't know what to make of it because we'd been taught, and believed, that when you die, you either go straight to heaven or hell. End of story. But we have found it isn't always like that. There are many trapped spirits, locked in a time warp, still active over the land.

On the occasion we'd been helicoptered into the mountains, we noticed for the first time that the trapped spirits were actually waiting for us with fascinated interest. In the morning as we were preparing for the day we had prayed down God's love and light over the area—so maybe it was His Light that had attracted them. But they were waiting, and I could see them amongst the trees around the edge of the clearing where the cabin was situated. I knew there had been a massacre in the area, as the Lord had told me there was 'much darkness' there, so I really wasn't surprised to 'see' the people.

We started ministry by asking God to forgive what mankind had done to mankind in the area. Sometimes we know the history of a place and can pray more specifically straight off, but most often we are waiting on the Lord. There had been much dishonour. We listened to the Holy Spirit and prayed more specifically against the driving forces that had caused the slaughter there. Things like domination and control, jealousy, hatred, fear, revenge and greed. We also asked God to forgive the worship of false gods in the place. We had Holy Communion, broke bread and shared 'the wine' and buried some of it in the ground in the centre of the clearing. The blood of Jesus cleanses the land from all things that have defiled it. Remember how the blood of Abel cried out from the ground for justice? So too does the blood of so many others cry out for vindication and justice.

We then called to these earthbound ones to come to Jesus. We told them who Jesus was and is, preaching the gospel of salvation to them. Since it is thought that Jesus Himself was the One who proclaimed the gospel to the dead (see 1 Peter 4:6), we are simply doing as He Himself did.

We always ask Jesus to come and receive them and He did—this time as the Lion of the Tribe of Judah. He frequently shows Himself as the Lion when the 'people' are the ancient inhabitants of the land, the ones whose forebears have been here since primeval times. It is interesting: they seem to know immediately who He is. Even though they worshipped ancestral deities, and even though they sacrificed their children to the powers of darkness, somehow they recognise the Lion.

This day, the Lion sat in the middle of the clearing, looking at the people. His gentle love radiated from His face. He was huge. I do not know why He chooses to show up one way one day and another way on another. He is the Lord; He doesn't have to explain this to us.

I will digress a moment to explain 'magnification'!

> One night when I was worshipping the Lord and talking to Him, He asked me again what I could see. I sat for a moment and I 'saw' two horses galloping side by side across a big plain towards the light of a city a great distance away. Actually I could only see the two horses' heads and necks from behind. Their necks strained as they galloped and their manes were flying back in the wind. I wasn't sure if my husband and I were the horses, or if we were riding them—one of the names the Lord gave to us through prophecy when we visited the Toronto Airport Church in 2012 was that we were his 'Belgian Blue Horses'. We were told the Belgian Blues were very strong, more so than the big Clydesdale horses we are used to. We had laughed to ourselves at the time; my husband had even joked we were more like 'old nags'—being well on in years—which brought a very sharp response from the Lord.

But the horses in my picture looked lighter than draught horses and galloped freely. Then I realised we were dressed in armour and were riding the horses. I looked for the Lord, but could not see Him, so I began talking to Him and praising Him. I asked Him where He was and then I saw Him as the Lion of Judah running ahead of us. The galloping horses were following Him. As I praised and worshipped Him, He became bigger and bigger as He ran ahead of us with His mane blowing in the wind. He told me that, when we praise and exalt Him, His presence grows in our midst. There are many references to magnifying the Lord in the Bible including Psalm 34:3. He was teaching me about the power of worship in warfare. Not long after this we were part of a 12-hour worship time in a church. Towards the end of this day a visitor stood up and said she had seen the Lion of Judah in the church and that He was so huge He could hardly fit into the big high area up the front of the building! She had no idea what the Lord had told me about magnifying Him in worship. Wow, I thought, and thanked Him as I laughed up into His face before sharing this story of the galloping horses.

Digression over! So the Lion called to the 'people' around the edge of the clearing with little grunts. I have seen Him do this many times and they responded by coming forward and throwing their arms around Him as they snuggled against His great hairy Alpha Male Lion chest. They held bunches of His mane in their hands as they pressed in against Him. I had never seen anyone grasp His mane in this manner before, but it seemed to be something specific to this group that day. They hung onto Him in sheer joy. It was beautiful. The 'children' always love Him and dance around Him with such absolute delight.

Then I noticed a much bigger 'person', standing out to one side. It was clear that, in his lifetime, he'd been part of 'the opposition'. He came diffidently forward. He wanted to approach Jesus too but he knew he was 'the enemy'. He was afraid he might be rejected.

The Lion held His great paw out to him and swept him into a huge embrace. The others moved over to give him space against the Lion's chest. There was no animosity—only love, forgiveness and acceptance. Once you have looked into the face of Jesus, into His beautiful eyes, in whatever form He chooses to take, all negativity rolls aside. The angels came and escorted this joyous band of 'people' away.

We thought that this must be the end of the ministry in this place, but suddenly I saw a newcomer. It was what we've come to call a 'weasel spirit' and it was entering the clearing near the side of the cabin. He was almost sneaking in. I guess he wanted to see what all the light and joyful cries were about. I called to him to come to Jesus.

This is an extremely important point to note: we *never* have discussions with these trapped human spirits and we *definitely do not* call up the dead—they are already there. We *do not* ask them questions—that is an aspect of necromancy. We just preach the gospel to them—though, exactly what form the gospel takes is led by the Holy

Spirit. If they have in fact been victims of human sacrifice, we tell them about Jesus who is the one true, pure, perfect sacrifice for the sin of the world. They understand sacrifice. We always tell them that Jesus is the only way out of this place of 'lostness' to the Father in heaven.[92] We listen to the Holy Spirit about what to say.

'Weasels' are usually ones who have run with the hares and hunted with the hounds. They have betrayed their own and then, having been betrayed in turn, met the same fate. They weasel and make excuses; they are full of self-pity, unforgiveness and shame. They can never see Jesus even when He is standing right in front of them. They are so full of their own misery and are often totally out of touch with their own sin. It is everyone else's fault!

The Lion was still sitting in the middle of the clearing, watching this man with such love. However, He never intervened. He always waits until they can see Him and choose to come to Him. I bound down many things like guilt, unforgiveness, betrayal, shame. These people actually hate themselves because of their cowardliness. They betrayed their friends and family in the hope of saving their own skin—but it sure didn't pay off for any of the ones we have seen. They met the same fate as those they betrayed.

On one occasion I was praying for a weaselling 'man' and he was finally able to see Jesus, who just looked at him with such serious love—this is not a mollycoddling syrupy love; Jesus is not like that. He doesn't say, 'There, there, don't cry, I forgive you,' but waits until they have got in touch with their stuff and understand their own sin and condition before Him. This 'weasel' finally got a true insight into himself and he wept. Then Jesus, with one look, restored his dignity and the 'man' was able to stand tall again. He understood who the Lord had created him to be and could go off with the Lord his head up, all shame and self-hate washed away in the blood of Jesus.

On this day in the mountains however, this 'man' whined and moaned and made up all manner of excuses. We didn't engage in dialogue with him—we never do—we just continued to tell him about Jesus as we prayed for Holy Spirit guidance about how to proceed. The man was about to skive off again into the bushes but we called him back and bound what was keeping his eyes closed to Jesus. Finally he was able to see Jesus—the Lion of Judah—still sitting in the middle of the clearing. Weasel ran to him and threw himself against that great hairy chest and sobbed and sobbed.

The Lord just quietly held him closely till his tears had abated. He too had been restored by the gentle love of the Lord and went off with Him. These things always bring tears to my eyes as I remember them. The love of the Lord is so amazing. It can soften the hardest, most angry, most deeply wounded hearts and bring them peace, healing and dignity.

We spent the night in the cabin and the following day walked out over a significant high point. Over almost twelve hours we walked up over the range and down the other side, stopping and ministering on the way as the Lord showed us.

Frequently as we walk in different localities we are not aware of any bird life. Then suddenly the Lord will send a bird or group of birds who come and chatter to us, attracting our attention. Sometimes the birds come after we have ministered and they sing a joyful 'thank you' to the Lord. But when they come unexpectedly out of the blue and chatter loudly, really getting in our faces, it means: 'Be aware, there is something here you need to see.' At one place, as we were going along a ridge, the birds were particularly garrulous. Maybe it was a threshold, even if it was not one of the obvious ones like a stream, a hill top or a gateway. We stopped, alert and watchful, feeling and listening, when suddenly I saw two or three largish 'spiritual snakes' slithering up the side of the hill towards us. They were coming very determinedly. We just bound them down and carried on.

Near the top of the hill we encountered more trapped spirits and followed a similar style of ministry to down at the cabin the day before. We were eventually able to claim that high point for the Lord. The Lion came and stood on high, wearing His victory crown and His royal banner flying over His shoulder. There was no denying who was Lord of this place, as His majestic voice roared out across the land.

And another digression! This time about the Lion's roar:

> A couple of days later His roar from another summit was totally different. As we had prayed in the misty cloud, repenting for the things mankind had done to mankind on this 'high place' and the region all around below, I 'saw' the Lion crouched just below the top of the highest point. I couldn't actually see the high point in the physical because of the mist. In fact, it had come in so thick and so fast that we could hardly see each other. I texted some of

our intercessors and some answered my text, and began to pray for us. In the spirit I could see the Lion—He was crouched down like a cat ready to spring, his tail twitching as He waited to leap up onto the top and take the 'critter' that was proudly strutting its stuff on top. We bound down the sins that could have given it licence to be there and, when I said, 'Domination and Control,' the Lion gave one mighty leap, landing on the proud but unsuspecting 'critter'. The Lion was so angry and tore the thing to shreds with His mighty claws. It was brutal; I have seen Him do this a few times and every time it is about something that really angers Him. He was very angry this time, ripping the 'critter' up. The angels had to come and take the mutilated thing away. Then the Lion stood and roared a great angry roar out across the land; there was no denying He was Lord and He was angrily telling the forces of darkness who was in control! Then He changed the sound into a long deep roar of yearning as He called all people unto Himself. Please don't ignore His invitation to you to come. It wasn't long after that that the mist cleared enough for us to see the actual physical high point, and we raced up there to claim it for the Lord. The prayers of our intercessor had been answered.

Back to the story in hand! We carried on up over the hill and as we were about to go into the bush on the other side, again a very urgent crying of a bird brought us to a standstill. We asked the Lord what it was about, and listened. I immediately 'saw' a giant lizard. My sister also discerned the 'lizard' presence and said so at the same time. This giant lizard was comparatively small when I think of others I have seen. It was only about three metres long. I have seen them around 14–18 metres long. This baby giant was running up the track towards us. We bound it down in Jesus' name and the angels took it away.

Later, the Lord called us to further prayer over the area, but this time from home. This often happens. My husband and I were shown two huge lizards, down by the confluence of the two streams where we had begun the mission. We have seen two like this quite often where there has been a big battle or massacre. They are big and angry and they come running towards us.

The first two I ever saw were huge—they looked like monster monitor lizards. One came racing along the beach towards me. I just bound it down, and the Lord speared it through its heart, killing it, and then the angels took it away. But then… as I sat looking up the beach, I couldn't believe my eyes. It looked like the same huge monstrous monitor lizard was running down the beach towards me again. I was confused and wondered if I had seen correctly the first time. I bound that one down and it met the same fate.

The Lord then told me there were indeed two of them, called 'Fear' and 'Ugly'. Now, when we discern there has been a battle where we are praying, I look out for 'Fear' and 'Ugly'—or their unholy cousins!

The other thing that we saw at this confluence was a big angry 'octopus'. We have learned to expect these where there has been human sacrifice into water. This particular 'octopus' came up the main stream towards us, its long legs flailing as it scrambled over the rocks. All of these 'critters' we bind down in Jesus' name, the Lord spears them through and the angels carry them off.

As far as we have been able to make out, these 'critters' are the manifestation of curses spoken by a witch doctor or occult practitioner. They seem to have been part of covenants with the underworld and the curses are directed against anyone coming against them in war. The underworld has probably been paid off with human sacrifice. It makes sense that we've seen the Lion shred the 'critters' with His claws— He's tearing up covenants with Death and with Sheol.

Curses were—and are—very powerful weapons thrown by the enemy. The poison they carry passes down the family line, generation after generation. When Jesus died on the cross, He broke the power of every curse! Curses have to be nailed to the cross to cancel their power on the land and on the people they were sent to destroy.

Final word! The Lord gave us Psalm 24:1-4 NIV as our mandate to walk the walk He has taken us on.

> *The earth is the Lord's, and everything in it, the world, and all who live in it...*
>
> *Who may ascend the hill of the Lord? Who may stand in His holy place?*
>
> *He who has clean hands and a pure heart, who does not give up his soul to an idol or swear by what is false.*

We cannot go on a 'mission' walking in dishonour. Well, we can, of course, but it is not going to go well! Galatians 5:19-21 gives us a checklist of attitudes to avoid. While we might not consciously be walking in some of these more overt strife-bringers, nevertheless jealousy, envy and anger can be very subtle. Ask Him for revelation: 'Am I walking in any dishonour towards You or anyone else, Lord?'

If He brings someone to mind, then repent of the disrespect you have shown towards them. And also ask Jesus to empower your words of repentance.

Stay sweet, stay sweet. Galatians 5:22–23 gives us the list of the Holy Spirit's beautiful sweet fruit to walk in.

> *'But the fruit of the Spirit is love, joy, peace, patience, kindness, goodness, faithfulness, gentleness and self-control. Against such things there is no law.'*

Amen.

Once to every man and nation comes the moment to decide
In the strife with Truth and Falsehood
for the good or evil side.

James Russell Lowell, 1845

Prayer

It is vitally important to recognise that prayer is about relationship with the Father. None of the prayers in this book are intended as a formula but as a guideline to help you realign yourself with the holy Trinity. They are meant as a starting point for a conversation.

Transformation is only possible as you hold onto the hem of Jesus' prayer shawl and ask Him to mediate before the Father for you. In the end, it's all about Him!

It's true, Lord, there comes a pivotal moment in life when the decision must be made between You and the enemy. The choice determines if we experience the peace, the *shalom*, that passes all understanding or if we continue to be plagued by setbacks beyond our understanding.

I confess to making the wrong choices, Lord. I've partnered with Resheph and the other threshold guardians. I've failed the test. And I've failed to take advantage of Your grace when You've presented me with extra chances to redo the test. The truth is simple: I've failed to make You the number one priority in my life.

When You've asked me to do unusual things, 'weird stuff', I've backed away in fear. I've only wanted to do the things that are 'normal' for my culture, 'safe' in my society—the sort of things that will effortlessly enhance both my reputation and my affluence—without any backlash or trouble.

I am sorry. I repent. Heavenly Father, Jesus made the way straight and clear for me, but I was too busy doing things I considered more important to notice. Father, forgive me my distraction and my blindness. Help me to see. Open my eyes to the wonder of Your world and the blessings that surround me.

Lord, teach me that, when I dishonour the earth I dishonour Your good gifts to me and I dishonour You. So I will reap dishonour. Teach me what it means to be a good steward of all You have entrusted to me. Help me, through the Fruit of the Spirit, to overcome the threshold guardians who block the way into my calling. Help me to pass the test—not so that life will be suddenly perfect but so that I can advance Your kingdom through the inheritance You have given to me. Help me to repent and heal the mess I have made of my regency of the part of the world You have given me.

In Jesus' name, I pray, Amen.

First century temple shekel with inscription,
Tyre Holy and Inviolable

5

The Harrowing

FANS OF *THE LORD OF THE RINGS* will probably recognise the inspiration behind the title of the last chapter. *The Paths of the Dead* is a short-cut that the Grey Company, headed by Aragorn, takes through a haunted pass in the White Mountains to reach southern Gondor before it is attacked by corsairs. Throughout fantasy and fable, folklore and mythology, there are tales of heroes who venture into the underworld. Orpheus, Odysseus, Castor and Pollux, Inanna, Tammuz, Nergal, Hercules, Adonis and Dionysius are just a few of the champions of legend who sank down to the world below and then returned alive. Some—the rare few—emerged unscathed. Most were, in some way, blighted by the experience.

There's a curious fact about these myths and legends. Jesus takes them seriously. He doesn't just dismiss them as unworthy of notice. He tackles them—earnestly and comprehensively. It's as if they've appropriated prophecy rightly belonging to Him and He refused to leave any stone unturned in returning it all to its rightful Owner.

Aragorn's actions, like those of Aslan as he revives the statues of the living dead in the White Witch's castle,[93] hark back to the creedal and theological understanding that Jesus descended into the realm of the dead and that He accomplished the 'harrowing of hell' by bringing out a triumphal procession of captives. This concept has long been understood to be implied by:

> *Therefore it says, 'When He ascended on high, He led captive a host of captives, and He gave gifts to men.' Now this expression, 'He ascended,' what does it mean except that He also had descended into the lower parts of the earth?*
>
> Ephesians 4:8–9 NASB

and

> *The gospel was proclaimed even to the dead, so that they might be judged indeed according to men in the flesh, but they might live in the spirit according to God.*
>
> 1 Peter 4:6 BLB

Who proclaimed the gospel to the dead? This verse has always been considered to refer to Jesus. (Many translations render the first part of this verse as 'proclaimed to those who are *now* dead' but that adds an interpretation which is not in the original Greek, suggesting it is only the living who can ever hear the gospel, and the idea that Jesus had gone to Sheol to liberate those who had died before His earthly coming is simply not a possibility. However the Greek word, 'katōtera', *lower parts*, is often used to refer to the underworld. Would God condemn those who had no chance to hear the gospel? Some would say 'yes', some 'no'.)

But I would say that the 'harrowing of hell' began even before the death and resurrection of Jesus. In a very real sense I would say it began with Lazarus. And I would further suggest that Bethany is not just a reference to *sorrow*, 'oni', but also obliquely to 'onah', *a deed of transfer*.

Chaim Bentorah says 'onah' sounds: 'a lot like *owner* which is what it means. To acquire the deed or title to a property. God becomes our owner, He acquires the deed of ownership from us. Well, before we are saved the enemy has a lien on that deed that must be satisfied before the transfer of the deed can be made… So, Jesus paid off the lien with His blood and now the deed of ownership of our soul passes to Jesus and we become His possession. He owns us, locks, stock, and barrel. If you don't like it you are free to spend eternity with some other owner. Like it or not we all have one of two possible masters. God or the enemy.'

A lien is the right to keep possession of property belonging to another person until a debt owed by that person is discharged. Jesus' purpose in going to Bethany was to declare that Resheph's rights—along with those of any other spiritual entity who claimed sovereignty in the underworld—were coming to an end. The debt was about to be paid off—not just for individuals, not just for the nation, but for the entire world. Saul's covenant with Death was, as God had long-promised, finally about to be annulled.

By the time I'd finished the third chapter of this book, I needed a break. Although I planned to work towards a climax featuring the comprehensive triumph of Jesus, I'd reached the stage where I felt so weighed down by gloom that I never wanted to think about Resheph or the underworld ever again. 'I've had enough,' I said to God. 'If You don't mind, I'm taking a vacation. I'm going to read something else.'

So I picked a promising-looking title from the many books in my to-be-read pile and settled back to enjoy a holiday from research. I was halfway through the second page—yes, just the *second* page!—when I realised my plans for time off were not going to materialise. The book was *The Ancient Paths* and it begins with a description of the Via Heraklea, the fabled route of the legendary Hercules across Celtic Europe. The great Carthaginian general, Hannibal, apparently followed the footsteps of this demi-god in his attack on Rome. He trekked up through Spain, across France, over the Alps and down into Italy, using solstice sunpaths for a guide. Or at least, so the book said.

Now more-or-less straight lines across large swathes of landscape: that sounded eerily like the kind of lines that Leviathan creates for itself, using the path-of-totality of eclipses or other natural tracks across the countryside. Leviathan and Hercules?! At first it seemed an oddball pairing. Yet the mention of Hannibal from the Phoenician colony of Carthage suggested that perhaps it was more appropriate to consider a Hercules other than the Roman and Greek one. I was, in fact, immediately reminded of Hercules Melqart. It took a few seconds for the shekel to drop: there's a famous gospel story about Hercules Melqart. Once again, it's about Jesus reacting to a godling of death. Melqart means *king of the city* and, throughout the ancient world, '*the city*' in question was universally recognised as the metropolis of the underworld.

Now you're probably thinking that you don't remember Hercules ever being mentioned in Scripture. You'd be absolutely right. The legendary strongman does not actually appear by name in the gospels. However he turns up in the most unexpected places. Perhaps, most surprisingly, in a fish's mouth! But he was also warmly welcomed into the precincts of the Temple.

During the time of Jesus, the Jewish people were forbidden by their Roman overlords to mint their own currency. This meant they had to import coins from outside the country. Now some foreign producers would engrave an image to the customer's requirements but others did not offer any choice. The priests in Jerusalem made the decision that, rather than accept any inferior metal, they would require the temple tax to be paid using silver coins of the highest quality sterling—a level of purity that could only be obtained from the mint in Tyre. But that was one of the places where no choice was offered about engraving: the shekels came stamped with an image of Hercules Melqart on one side and, on the other, an eagle surrounded by the words, 'Tyre, Holy and Inviolable'.

The irony of choosing pure metal but not keeping the Temple sanctum pure is inescapable. There's blatant exaltation of the old Phoenician mother-city as holy, along with contempt of God's commandment forbidding graven images. No wonder Jesus called them hypocrites: they forced people to mock God by paying tribute through immaculate silver that flouted His law.

Still this was about profit—about *greed* and *desire*, the very words that lurk in the background of 'keseph', the Hebrew word for *silver* or *money*. But 'kasaph', *greed*, *longing*, *shame*—not to forget the resonance of *being eclipsed*—also contains a very significant element: 'saph', meaning *threshold*. The 'prince of Tyre'—the very spirit cast out of heaven[94] for trading—had moved shop, right into the foyer of the Temple in Jerusalem. It was obscene enough to use a likeness of Melqart—known more commonly to the Jews as Moloch, the fire-idol who demanded child sacrifice—on the only coins that could be used to pay the temple tax. But the priests made the situation more heinous still by setting up currency traders on the Temple threshold. Ordinary worshippers were forced to exchange their regular money for silver shekels at exorbitant rates.

Yes, it's the famous episode where Jesus made a whip and began overturning the tables of the money-changers. As they fled, no doubt taking their scattered shekels with them, they unwittingly enacted a prophecy.[95] Jesus emptied the Temple of the image of Death—six days later, He would empty the tomb of Death itself.[96]

Two thousand years later, neither Hercules nor Death has ever truly lost their association with money. A mortgage is literally a 'death pledge'. And no one is totally sure why the symbol for a dollar started out as a capital S with two vertical bars through it, but one long-standing suggestion is that the two vertical bars represent the Pillars of Hercules: the two promontories that flank the Strait of Gibraltar and that marked the 'end of the world' for Phoenician traders.[97] Double pillars were such an important part of temple architecture for the Phoenicians it is no surprise that Solomon's Temple—built with the aid of the Phoenicians of Tyre under the direction of Hiram—was fronted by the pillars, Boaz, *strong one*, and Jachin, *he will establish*.[98]

In the earliest Canaanite temples, the 'mazzebah' or *pillar* represented the deity and was an object of worship.[99] So perhaps it's not unexpected to find money still associated with an ancient symbol of a pillar or two, given the adulation of mammon in our current age. And it's also worth remembering that money-changers in the temple of Jesus' day would have been stationed close to the entrance pillars.

Boaz is related to names like Uzzah, *strength*, and Uzziah, *God is my strength*. Erik Langkjer suggests that a more accurate meaning of Boaz may be *the morning star*. He indicates that Bo'az is probably cognate with 'Azizu, *strong one*, an Arabic name for *the morning star*.[100]

The related Hebrew word, 'ayil', is heavily contextualised—depending on the background to its use, it can mean *pillar, ox, stag, oak, ram, mighty man* and, yes, even *morning star*. The conceptual link between all these disparate things is that each one of them is, within its own kind, *a strong leader*.

Thus it wasn't too great a stretch for the ancient mind to associate both Boaz, *strong one*, and Hercules, the strongman, with prominent pillars. In fact, it was hardly a stretch at all.

But let's not forget that Lazarus, especially in its older Hebrew form, Eleazar, contains that element for *strength*, 'az', even if it's been modified a bit to mean *support*. Yet this name points to a different source, to God as the giver of strength.

Whenever Jesus pitted Himself against Resheph—whether it was as Hercules Melqart or any other guise—we find these thematic links about true strength. '*Love is as strong as Death*,' Solomon had said in the Song of Songs.

No, said Jesus. *Not at all. That's to seriously underrate Love.* So the song of Jesus is wondrously, marvellously different: 'Love is as strong as My Abba.'

The sisters Mary and Martha had immensely important roles to play in the ongoing conflict against Resheph. The raising of Lazarus wasn't a single once-for-all-time knockout blow to the enemy. It was instead a major engagement in an ongoing war of 'herem': one devoted to total destruction.

In particular, Mary's appointment was extremely significant. As I have indicated in *Dealing with Ziz*, I believe the evidence very strongly indicates that Mary of Bethany, the sister of Lazarus and Martha, is also Mary Magdalene. She therefore not only anointed Jesus as the Son of David for His ride through Jerusalem on a donkey—just as Solomon, the son of David, had ridden a donkey through Jerusalem to his coronation—she was the witness selected to remember the details of both the death and resurrection of the Lord. She was the 'kingmaker' who anointed and washed the Kingly Messiah, she was the 'watcher' who observed the sacrifice of the Priestly Messiah and she was the 'mountain-builder' who helped prepare the mountain of spices for the final battle of the War Messiah.

She also had seven demons at one point. Just as God chose demon-afflicted Saul as the first king of Israel, He chose a broken woman as the representative of His Bride. When she spoke to Jesus in the garden, her words echo the wedding scene from the Song of Songs. Did she go to anoint a dead body or did she believe Jesus would return from the dead? If anyone did, surely it was this woman who had seen Lazarus raised to life after four days in the tomb.

Arie Uittenbogaard makes a compelling case that John described the raising of Lazarus in great detail precisely so any Gentile reader would receive a swift education in Jewish burial customs and realise that, when it came to Jesus, there were some serious anomalies to be noted.

'Lord, by this time he stinketh!' protested Martha when Jesus asked for the tomb of Lazarus to be opened.[101] What!? Stinketh? No myrrh? No spices?

No indeed. In our modern tradition we've normalised the burial of Jesus, reading into what happened the idea that the use of aromatic oils and embalming spices was more-or-less common practice—when the gospels themselves testify otherwise. The presence of myrrh in His tomb was excessively unusual.[102] Nonetheless there was considerable first century ritual involving the use of myrrh. But it involved weddings, not funerals.

John's gospel emphasises those faithful who, by their presence at the crucifixion, were finally in a position to realise what John the Baptist had meant when he said Jesus was the Bridegroom. Most likely Nicodemus was the first to grasp the ramifications of Jesus' last word. Let's face it—no one keeps a million dollars' worth of myrrh in storage. At today's prices, that's how much he provided! Mary had been savagely criticised less than a week previously for her extravagance in anointing Jesus with one-hundredth of what Nicodemus supplied. He'd have had to have sent out his servants to buy up myrrh everywhere and anywhere they could find it.

Nicodemus was there apparently to hear the last cry of Jesus and watch the centurion drive a spear into His side. He'd seen the blood and water gushing out. He was a teacher in Israel, a highly respected and intelligent man capable of putting two and two together and coming up with the right answer.

We are told that, in Greek, the last word of Jesus was, 'Tetelestai!' *It is accomplished, it is finished, it's complete, it's done, it is fulfilled, it is consummated*: these are the meanings and resonances of 'tetelestai'.

However, an Aramaic word with the same overtones, 'kallah', had still further resonances. For the Jews, 'kallah' was the jubilant cry of a bridegroom at the consummation of a marriage. It had the further sense, '*My bride!*'

Traditionally a bridegroom in Israel was anointed with an aromatic lotion called 'oil of joy'. What was 'oil of joy'? It was myrrh.

Nicodemus, in a truly spectacular display of faith, stepped up and fulfilled the position left vacant by the death of John the Baptist. He became the 'Friend of the Bridegroom' and rushed to supply myrrh for the wedding. He clearly got the implications: not just of Jesus' last word but also of the blood and water that flowed from His pierced side.[103] Blood and water come at a birth. But spirit and water accompany the 'new birth'. That's what Jesus had told him during his clandestine visits.

Now the Greek word for *blood* also means *spirit*. So Nicodemus would have recognised the 'new birth' occurring as blood and water flowed from the spearwound—but, still, he would have also realised it's simply not normal for anyone to be born from the pierced side of a man. It just never happened. Well, *almost* never. There was a time in history, just once, when it had occurred previously—when the bride of the first man, Adam, had been taken from the place in his side just under his heart. Nicodemus would have realised he had witnessed something as momentous as the birth of Eve. There was a wedding coming and he needed to play his part in a history-making celebration.

As did Mary. Because she was the God-appointed representative of the Bride of Christ.

So complex and intricate was Mary's role in the healing of history it's wise to step back a little, so that we can take a wider cultural snapshot of what happened in the garden outside the tomb. Hercules—yes, unfortunately, we're back to Hercules—is a constellation. It happens to contain a point called the 'solar apex' which is the position in the sky that the solar system is travelling towards.[104] Now the present group of stars we call 'Hercules' wasn't always known by that name. Previously it was dubbed 'Engonasin', *kneeling man*, and prior to that, it was known to the Greeks, and probably the Sumerians as well, as *the hind* or *the stag*.[105]

It happens that the Hebrew word for *kneel* is 'barak', which also means *blessing* and *lightning*. There's a neat segue of ideas here: *stag, kneel, lightning*—all wrapped up in a star figure. Both *stag* and *lightning* are iconic symbols of Resheph. And so perhaps is a *star*.

Resheph was not only pictured with the horns of a gazelle or a deer, it was also known as the 'door-warden of the sun'—the one who opened the door for the sun goddess as she descended into the underworld via the darkness of the west. This description suggests the evening star.

But the evening star is the morning star. As we've seen, the name Boaz may be a reference to that 'strong leader' of the morning. The official Hebrew name for the morning star is exceptionally beautiful: 'ayelet hashachar', *the deer at the dawning of the day*.[106]

This phrase is a musical notation, perhaps the name of an ancient tune, and it's found in the heading to Psalm 22. This song of David, quoted by Jesus as He was dying, is once again a reference to Resheph that is subtle, indirect and allusive. But after a while the sheer number of subtle, indirect and allusive links start to approach critical mass. Even so, the mass is tangled and difficult to unravel because we have to keep moving back and forward across different eras and different cultures to understand even a fraction of the totality of Jesus' ransacking of the underworld.

As we've seen Hercules Melqart was a solar deity, allegedly associated with the Via Heraklea, a track with a bearing aligned to the angle of the sun at the summer solstice. This ancient way is said to have followed basically a straight trajectory across half a continent from the western edge of Spain to the Swiss Alps. It is highly reminiscent of the path of totality of a solar eclipse.[107] Both eclipses and sun-lines are associated with Leviathan, as are other lines in the landscape.

Hannibal's route to Rome with his armies and elephants deliberately followed the path of Hercules. While there is unquestionably a clever strategy in coming at Rome through the back-door, Hannibal's motivation was apparently more religious than military. It's the long, long, long, long, long, long scenic way around when it would have been possible to land his fleet in Italy. Hannibal seems to have wanted to have been seen as the new Hercules: the invincible strongman who could claim divine descent. He might have wanted the mantle but he also wanted the blessing; so he aligned himself with the part-human sun-god by following in his footsteps along an old and sacred path.

Jesus Himself did something very similar: in going from Bethany-beyond-the-Jordan to Bethany, He began His battle strategy by retracing the path of Saul's bones as they were moved from Jabesh Gilead to Zela at David's behest. In addition to undoing Saul's covenant with the underworld, Jesus was also repairing the covenant breach between the House of David and the House of Saul—a breach caused by David's actions which gave

Resheph, the godling of death and killing heat, even further legal right.

Now I want to stress, by stating the life of Jesus shows forth similar mythic, folkloric, legendary and fantasy elements to the tales of Hercules and Hannibal, that I do not mean for even a single second to imply the gospel record is not a factual account. On the contrary. It's true. True in the ordinary sense of truth, understood for thousands of years by countless people—not in any relativistic, post-post-modern sense. Jesus is the Way, the Truth and the Life and the only route to the Father.

So why do these confusing parallels exist?

Along the millennia, signs in the heavens, wonders in nature, the covenantal promises of God, the utterances of the prophets, even the shape of history itself—all these things—pointed to the Son who would be incarnate in Jesus. So Leviathan—king of a brood of 'young lions', the sons of pride—had ample opportunity to slot all the jigsaw pieces together far better than humanity ever could. Although it would not be possible to do so perfectly, Leviathan could conspire with the various principalities of the nations to foreshadow our Saviour in various guises. There was, after all, a prophecy about a stag and a garden:

> *'O you who sit in the gardens,*
> *My companions are listening for your voice—*
> *Let me hear it!'*
>
> *'Hurry, my beloved,*
> *And be like a gazelle or a young stag*
> *On the mountains of spices.'*

Song of Songs 8:13–14 NASB

Leviathan might not have known what the outworking of this particular and spectacular prophecy would look like when the Messiah came as the *strong leader*, the Firstborn from the Dead. In fact, not even those destined to create the 'mountain of spices'—Nicodemus, Mary, Mary and Mary, as well as Joseph of Arimathea—had any idea in advance. They clearly didn't understand how the *Parable of the Wise and Foolish Bridesmaids* applied to them.

But Leviathan had a few clues. It knew there would be a war to the death, so it tried very hard to defile the image of the 'deer in the garden' centuries before Jesus arrived on the scene.

In his high fantasy adventure, *The Voyage of the 'Dawn Treader'*, CS Lewis introduced Eustace Clarence Scrubb to *The Chronicles of Narnia*. Right at the beginning of the story, we're informed that Eustace was so odious in his behaviour he 'almost deserved' his name. Now I'm not so sure the name actually is odious, but it certainly is odd. And I say that because, throughout the old folklore Lewis was steeped in, the name 'Eustace' was connected with a deer, not with a dragon.

In a pivotal episode in the story, Eustace falls asleep in the cave of a dying dragon, while thinking dragonish thoughts. When he wakes up, he discovers he's been transformed into a dragon. Now personally I'd have thought, given his name and given the motifs of repentance and baptism that follow, it would have been a stag. Yet, throughout the scenes with Eustace, there's a merger of symbols connected on the one hand with Leviathan the dragon and, on the other, with Resheph the stag. When Eustace is finally undragoned by the Great Lion, Aslan, the scene involves a bright morning star, a garden and a well. The armband that Eustace acquires suggests a covenant symbol—in cultures where the shedding of blood is abhorred, bracelets and armbands substitute for the 'cut' of covenant.[108] Another hint of Resheph is found later in the story, when a fire-berry of the sun brought to Ramandu (a name perhaps related to 'ramad', *scorcher*) is likened to a burning coal.

Such stories remind us that, while over the last few centuries there's been a steady demythologising of the Scriptures in order that spirits like Resheph and Ziz, Belial and even Python are depersonalised into mild abstractions, God has continued to inform His people of their existence. Sure, it's been fantasy fiction where He's been active in revealing the truth about these entities—but that is in perfect keeping with one of the oldest meanings of the word 'fantasy': *truth made visible.* He has not been silent.

As belief in the spiritual world has ebbed and flowed, we have lost a great deal of understanding of what the Bible says about the guardian spirits of thresholds, as well as the principalities and world-rulers who partner with them. Even when we still retain a belief in God, our view of Him is impoverished by our failure to see how He has overcome them in the ordinary ups and downs of everyday life.

> *You believe that there is one God. Good! Even the demons believe that—and shudder.*
>
> James 2:19 NIV

Leviathan-Resheph not only believes in God. It also believes in prophecy. Like us, it has a Book chockfull of prophecies but, unlike us, it has had an eon to study them and to tease out all the enigmatic nuances. Leviathan-Resheph also has an additional advantage: it hasn't been hampered by translations that obscure the densely layered allusions, the rich and poetic evocations or the possible alternative renderings of the original language.

As we noted in the first chapter, Scripture is considered to contain four levels:

- **Pashat** = *plain*.
- **Remez** = *hint*.
- **Derash** = *inquiry*.
- **Sod** = *secret*.

We've already seen the multiplicity of options available to identify 'ayil': *oak, pillar, stag, ox, ram, chief*—anything that, of its kind, could be considered a *strong leader*.

Let's look at another example to get a better feel for these levels. The following example is far from random; it has a tangential relation to several matters we've discussed so far. Jeremiah was mourning the devastation of Jerusalem in an interesting passage that hints of the inhabitants trying to magically control the seraphim[109] when he asked:

> '*Is there no balm in Gilead? Is there no physician there?*'
>
> Jeremiah 8:22 NIV

Gilead, of course, is the territory where Jabesh Gilead was located. In Hebrew, 'Gilead' is spelled the same way as 'Galeed', *witness-heap*, the memorial of stones that Laban and Jacob built after their reconciliation in the region of Gilead. Basically its meaning is a *pile of rocks*. Gilead was not exactly the world's most fertile spot; it was here, in a place called Lo Debar, *no bread*, that Saul's lame grandson Mephibosheth[110] lived during the early days of David's reign. Gilead was rocks, rocks and more rocks.[111] But in this inhospitable terrain grew hardy trees that exuded a prized aromatic resin with renowned healing properties.

This famous Balm of Gilead is first mentioned in Scripture when Joseph was sold to the Midianite traders who were on their way to Egypt with a caravan of 'tsori', *balm*, 'lot', *myrrh* and 'nekot', *spice* or *aromatic gum*. Now 'tsori' is not only *balm*, it's also the word for a *person from Tyre*, the Phoenician mother-city. Since Tyre means *the rock* and was synonymous with trading, Jeremiah's question reeks of sarcasm. Instead of '*Is there no balm in Gilead?*' it could be: '*Are there no rocks in a pile of stones?*' But the further overtones are: '*Are there no traders east of the Jordan?*' In every case, the question is basically rhetorical and the answer 'no'.[112]

A certain mystery surrounds the motivation behind Jeremiah's question. It almost seems to come out of nowhere. Many commentators have therefore seen the 'Balm of Gilead' as a title of Jesus, the ultimate Healer. While I agree, let me nonetheless invoke the 'Law of First Mention' to guide us regarding the nuances of this phrase. This interpretative principle is by no means universally agreed upon, but it is a valuable way to examine Hebrew words. Besides, all my writings are in one way or another about thresholds, so a failure to look at the way a word is first used in Scripture is a subtle way of avoiding a threshold!

Now, as already mentioned, the first appearance of Balm of Gilead occurs when Joseph is sold as a slave. His brothers pull him out of a pit and do a trade with their cousins, the Midianites and the Ishmaelites. Yes, their *cousins*. This of course means they were Joseph's cousins too. The entire extended family was in on the betrayal. Joseph, the captive who would eventually be named Zaphenath-Paneah, *saviour of the world*, would have been tied, chained or bound in some way and probably stashed away with the baggage. All the way down to the 'underworld' of Egypt he'd have been kept with the other trade goods. After a few days, the aroma of balm and myrrh would have clung to his clothes.

Here we see a small but significant prophecy of the life of Jesus. As a baby He'd have gone to Egypt with gold, frankincense and myrrh. However in His last week, the fragrance of the myrrh Mary splashed on Him—during His anointing as king—would have clung to His clothes the entire time. He'd have been in the pit at the palace of Caiaphas, having been traded for thirty pieces of silver (as compared to Joseph whose brothers got twenty silver pieces for hoisting him out of a similar pit), with the aroma of myrrh and spikenard all over Him. Later, of course, Nicodemus spent a crazy amount of money on myrrh for the tomb.

And although it was oil of joy for a wedding, it was also embalming material for a burial. The Jews, however, didn't embalm bodies. That's the point of mentioning Martha's protest about the stench of decay. The presence of what would, under normal circumstances, be enough oil for half a dozen deceased Pharaohs again points back to Joseph who 'saved the world' from famine. But Joseph in turns points forward to Jesus, the true Saviour of the World.

Joseph ruled over Egypt, symbolic of the underworld for the Hebrews. For much of its history, the nation was under the aegis of green-faced Osiris, lord of the underworld and judge of the dead. Joseph's power over 'the underworld' pre-figures and prophesies of Jesus who would show what that kind of power truly meant. Osiris: is that who is really sovereign in the afterlife?

Before He raised Lazarus from the dead, Jesus said to Martha:

> *'I AM the Resurrection and the Life. Whoever believes in Me, though he die, yet shall he live, and everyone who lives and believes in Me shall never die. Do you believe this?'*
>
> John 11:25–26 ESV

This is one of seven 'I AM' sayings of Jesus. They are not simply claims to be divine; they are recalls on the usage rights to particular titles. Various godlings had usurped the titles of God and Jesus systematically took them back. In this instance, He was retrieving the 'Resurrection and the Life' from Osiris. However, don't get the idea Osiris is a counterpart of Resheph. That is Osiris' enemy, Set, who is widely regarded as a sovereign of the underworld.[113]

Yet early Christianity was unrelenting in its opposition to Osiris in ways that are rarely noticed. According to Plutarch, a high priest of Python Apollo,[114] the Pythagorean sect abhorred the number 17 because Osiris was killed on the seventeenth of the month by his enemy Set. He was dismembered, and because the last piece could never be found, he could not be re-integrated.

However 17 is *the* number of Christianity, favoured repeatedly in the literary structure of the gospels and epistles. It subverts the Pythagorean rejection of the number and embraces it both as the 'number of resurrection' and of 'spiritual government'.[115]

In another subversion, oil of myrrh—used to anoint the corpse of Osiris—was also in use at the tomb of Jesus. But it was not for embalming, nor for a burial; instead, it was to show what God had really designed it for: the celebration of a wedding.

'Unwrap him,' Jesus said of Lazarus.

Jesus was, at times, exceedingly provocative. I suppose, however, there's not much point in being subtle when war is being declared. So, although He could have chosen to ask His disciples about their perception of His identity just about anywhere and anywhen, the selection of the Gates of Hell in Caesarea Philippi on the Day of Atonement makes a statement that's hard to miss. The 'Gates of Hell'—or more specifically, Hades—was considered to be an underworld entrance at the shrine of the Greek goat-demon Pan. Now Pan, a threshold spirit of rejection and panic, is not strictly a spirit of the underworld. But, as the proximity of the Gates of Hell indicate, it is one of its strongest allies.

Hades, the Greek godling of the underworld was called Pluto by the Romans. He was also known as 'Dis'.[116] It is no coincidence in my view that 'dis' in English is so inseparable from the troubles of life. Disease, disrespect, disgrace, dispossess, disinherit, disappoint, dishearten, discontent, disenfranchise, distrust, disillusion, disintegrate, discriminate, disassociate, dismember, discourage, disparage, disadvantage, disconsolate, discredit, disfigure, disorder, disconnect, dismantle, discomfort, disagree, disable, disapprove, disdain, dislocate, disband, dishonest, disqualify... and on and on and on.[117]

In so many ways, each of these 'dis' words speaks of an aspect of death. They point to the sorrows of life which, so often—indeed far more often than we'd like to admit—we choose to make worse through complicity with Leviathan-Resheph. Like the tribe of Benjamin, wounded and hurt by those we expected to protect us, we wrap ourselves more securely in a covenant with Death and pull our grave clothes tighter through dishonour (yes, another of those 'dis' words!) of God and disobedience (and still another!) to His Word.

'Unwrap him,' Jesus said of Lazarus, 'and let him go.'

It's a command we have to ask our Lord to speak over us too. We can't get ourselves out of the clutches of Resheph-Leviathan. We need the power of Jesus to do that. We need Him to cut up our covenant with Death—for, if we do it ourselves, we will find innumerable sorrows and troubles descending on us for covenant violation.

The crossing of a threshold, so that we pass over into our destiny and calling, is always about coming out of the tomb. When we look at what Jesus Himself faced—the guard outside the entrance, the stone blocking the doorway, the curses affixed to the governor's seals—we see our own issues as well. But there is also the matter of unwrapping of the bonds confining us mentally, emotionally, physically, spiritually.

This is where other believers are needed, because we cannot unwrap ourselves. But most of us, in our pride, still want to do it without help. Pride keeps us wrapped up, complicit with Leviathan—whose name in Syrian religion, Lotan, means *the monster of the deep who wraps and twists*.

Prayer

It is vitally important to recognise that prayer is about relationship with the Father. None of the prayers in this book are intended as a formula but as a guideline to help you realign yourself with the holy Trinity. They are meant as a starting point for a conversation.

Transformation is only possible as you hold onto the hem of Jesus' prayer shawl and ask Him to mediate before the Father for you. In the end, it's all about Him!

Abba Father, I am just like Lazarus. I am spiritually, mentally, emotionally and physically bound. I am held captive by bonds of my own making, as well as by bonds others have placed on me. I am helpless—my face is covered and my eyes are unseeing. My hands and feet are tied but I know I am reaping what I have sown and what my generations have sown.

I have longed to unwrap myself and start again but I can't do that. I admit it, Lord—I can't do what I can't do and I am at the end of my own doings. But I can come before You and ask Jesus to speak on my behalf as I say to Him and to You: 'I repent, Jesus, for doing things my way. I repent of turning aside from You and of thinking I knew better than You. I repent of thinking You had forgotten me and my needs. Please forgive me and say, just as You did of Lazarus, *'Unwrap ... and let ... go.'*

Thank You, Jesus.

Already I feel the wind of the Spirit in my hair. I sense new spring and life in my step. My eyes blink to see more of the beauty of Your world. My ears are opened to hear the melody of birdsong all around. My taste is refreshed to relish delicious morsels in new ways.

Thank You, Lord Jesus, for enabling me to pass from death in order to experience life in new and miraculous ways. Thank You for walking the paths of the dead for me! Thank You for honouring me, even when I dishonoured You, even when I dishonoured Your Father and mine, even when I dishonoured the Holy Spirit! Lord, remove that deathly stench of dishonour from me and teach me how to worship You with nobility, joy and reverence. Show me how to glorify Your name and lift it high over my nation and beyond.

In Jesus' name. Amen.

6

The Author and Finisher

WHEN I WAS IN MY EARLY TWENTIES, I became involved in summer missions. Within just a few years, I'd been invited to co-lead the biggest team in the state. Since these were the days when I still appallingly shy, careful, cautious and hesitant, I asked the leader—who also happened to be the local director of a large international evangelistic organisation—why he was picking me. I pointed out several much better choices, just in case he'd overlooked them. And I wondered how he'd missed noticing how broken and depressed I was and how close to a complete breakdown.

'Don't take this wrongly,' he said. 'But I don't need you. I don't need anyone. I can run this show on my own. But the rules state I need to have a female co-leader, so if I have to have someone, I want someone I can trust in a crisis. That's the only time I need someone. So I want a co-leader who isn't going to fall apart but is going to step up to the plate and do whatever needs to be done. You look like a shy and retiring nobody, but you're not. If I hadn't seen you take charge when everyone else was going to pieces, I wouldn't have believed it.'

I was startled to realise that, even in my shattered condition, I had something to offer. Perhaps something valuable. The incident he referred to where 'everyone went to pieces' had happened the previous summer.

It was late afternoon, long slanting shadows providing welcome relief from the heat of the day. I'd been heading over to the dining hall because I was on roster to set tables for the evening meal when the director had intercepted me. 'Can you start getting dinner ready?' He was unpegging some tea-towels from a clothes line. 'The cook's had a bit of a meltdown. She had a vision of demons, flapping in these tea-towels, and she's in a bit of a hysterical state.'

I ducked around the clothes-line and stepped into the kitchen, only to find nothing whatsoever had been prepared. It was just ten minutes until the entire team was due to arrive! So I looked in the fridge and the pantry and decided on a menu—spaghetti bolognaise with fruit salad and ice cream. I didn't tell anyone I'd never cooked spaghetti bolognaise in my life because I figured I'd soon get help from someone who knew how and I'd be able to hand over the job. But it didn't work that way. The director made the mistake of telling the next three people the same thing he'd told me and they too joined the cook in a bit of a meltdown. After that he wised up and just gave them the basic instruction to help me out in the kitchen. Soon I was throwing commands left and right—you slice the onions, you grate the cheese, you chop the herbs, you cook the mince, you prepare the sauce, you cut up the fruit. A bare twenty minutes late, sixty people sat down to a substantial meal—and it seemed highly probable we'd be able to start the public evening programme right on time.

I went to chat with the cook because I knew she'd be feeling pretty bad. As I calmed her down, I was struck by a bizarre thought about those demon-infested tea-towels. 'I think she's intercepted a message meant for me.' That night, I had a curious dream—it was about witches and clothing in a wardrobe—and when I woke up, I said to myself, 'How strange! I used to have that nightmare all the time. But I don't think I've had it for about fifteen years.' God had indeed sent me a message. The memory of what happened when I was six had not yet emerged into the full light of day, but now there was a conscious link, through the kitchen incident, to a nightmare I'd had when I was six.

In the intervening years, I'd become—all unknown to myself—'parentally inverted' when it came to the occult. Put me in a situation where there was the faintest whiff of something untoward in the supernatural, I'd slam up boundaries, I'd become uncharacteristically assertive as I questioned authority, I'd take charge, I'd take over and I'd draw a non-negotiable line in the sand. Looking back, I can say with a fair degree of confidence that, had it been any kind of crisis other than occult-related, the director would never have seen the commanding officer in my personality break out into the open. It was all about damage control: I wasn't willing to risk other people making the same kind of mistake I had. I may not have known how to resolve my own situation but I had a fair few clues about how to avoid being caught in similar traps.

Fast-forward two decades and, by the time I'd hit my forties, I'd realised something was radically wrong in my life. My complete inability to come into what I felt was God's calling was perplexing. But I had absolutely no idea what was causing the problem. There were hints from God but they were so baffling, they were off-the-charts weird. I couldn't make any logical sense of them. And, pushing rational understanding to the side, the only feelings I could get in touch with about the nature of the wrongness were 'dispossession' and 'captivity'. Neither of those things made any real sense.

So, deeply frustrated, I decided to talk to my parents about it. Fortunately, neither of them had the slightest clue what I was talking about. In struggling to understand what I was saying, my mother somehow got the impression I thought they hadn't protected me when I was a child. So they started to apologise for something that happened around Christmastime when I was six years old. As they asked my forgiveness—even though they were in no way at fault—I was puzzled. It was apparent they were describing far and away the most significant event of my childhood... but I had no memory of it. None at all.

And then it started to come back in terrifying flashbacks. But remembrance returned only up to a point. Over several weeks, with my mother's help, I was able to reconstruct what had happened on that Boxing Day up until the time I'd left the room without her. And then there was nothing. It didn't matter how hard I tried to hammer on that door and open wide the memory regarding what had occurred after that, it was an impenetrable barrier. Beyond a certain point, there was nothing but a blank.

Months went by. The more I tried to push for total recall, the stronger and more intense the blankness became. But God had, unknown to me, been preparing the way for a very long time. During the two decades before this, I'd read hundreds of fantasy books. They'd had the fortunate effect of instilling in my heart an unassailable belief in a happily-ever-after. Sooner or later, I *knew* God would come through. He was clearly taking His time but, as George MacDonald[118] had pointed out, He is the one who calls all times 'soon'. Hope deferred was making my heart truly sick, but the belief in all things ending well had not eroded away. It was getting incredibly thin but it was still there. Just.

Now in the year or so prior to this, I'd turned from fantasy to non-fiction, especially reference works on folklore and mythology. So it was, in the Lord's great providence, that as I continued my reading of the legends from northern Europe, I came across a mysterious word in the Old Norse language. As soon as I encountered it, it flew straight into a lock in my mind and turned in the slot like a key. The door of memory flung open and there I was, six years old, sitting behind a rack of coats and dresses, listening to an enchanting whisper. 'If you concentrate hard enough, you can have anything you want.'

The word that opened the floodgates of memory was 'oskmær', *wishmaiden*. This dark spirit is allegedly an attendant of the Norse wargod, Odin,[119] similar to a valkyrie, those deathmaidens who were *choosers of the slain*.[120] Opportunistically trying to use a trauma to tempt me to make a wish that would cause me to covenant with it as its *chosen child, adopted one, beloved*—for these words are also meanings of 'oskmær'—it had been caught in its own trap. Because I had inadvertently used the power of one of its own names against it. And that name was 'Hel'.

Yes, a hell-spirit and I were hostages to one another. All of the hints God had given me over the years made perfect sense. All of the nightmares—and there were many different cycles of them—fitted together. All of the uneasy feelings I'd had for so long about 'harmless wishes' were suddenly explicable. The mess was so tangled and thorn-ridden that, even when I finally realised and turned the whole thing over to Jesus to fix, it took a long time for Him to work through it. It wasn't instant. Even today, many long years later, there are still aspects I struggle with, and that from time to time I find hidden away. There are errant emotions I have difficulty in daily surrendering to Him. Hell—Sheol—is the insatiable consumer. The restless tension I feel between consumption and contentment is ongoing. The sudden sense that I have to 'consume' something—and yet don't really want to—can strike at any time. I am looking forward to the time I can say as Paul did:

> *I have learned the secret of being content in any and every situation.*
>
> Philippians 4:12 NIV

Or at least not having my sense of contentment continually disturbed by an uneasy sense I'm in need of something to consume. I am so deeply grateful to Jesus that He has enabled us all, through His cross and resurrection, to receive the benefits of His annulment of any covenant with Death or agreement with Sheol. I can also truly say that, whatever your mess, whatever dark, unholy covenant is coming down your family line, He can sort it. And if you don't believe in a happy ending to your life story, He can sort that too.

There are some lines we should simply never cross. In all those decades I was in a stand-off with a wishmaiden, that's one thing I learned very quickly. I might not have known how to get out of the trap, but I became quite sensitive to unhelpful spiritual advice. Sometimes my instinct told me that the encouragement I was receiving to pray in particular ways would make the situation infinitely worse. It's all too easy to feel pressured into following the example of well-meaning believers who feel able to pray with boldness and freedom. It's difficult to resist that pressure. Countless times I asked myself: 'Who am I to argue with people who've been in the faith so much longer than I have?'

But once I'd renounced my false refuges and God had cancelled my covenant with Death, and I'd passed over the threshold into my calling, I instantly started to pray differently. I didn't need to think about it; it happened effortlessly. So I remain deeply conscious of not urging people to pray in any way that makes them feel uncomfortable. We don't know what constraints exist in their lives. Even now I haven't felt free to adopt any of the prayer protocols I found unhelpful in the past. They've remained off-limits. That hasn't changed.

Back during the time when I was co-leading on summer missions, there were times when spiritual lines were crossed. Two incidents stand out in my mind. On these occasions, the team had spontaneously gathered around a piano to worship God. One song gave way to another and, after about twenty minutes of buoyant camaraderie, the songs became funnier and sillier. Nothing wrong with that. Except that they quickly degenerated and developed a mocking edge.

The issue in these circumstances is not that we cross the line—because we're always going to fail. It's that we don't take hold of God's offer of grace to repent. The first time this happened I called the team back to order. It was a hard, hard thing to dampen the merriment and put a check on the bubbling hilarity. In fact, it was so difficult emotionally that, two years later, when an almost identical incident happened, I couldn't face doing it again. One of the long-term team members who'd been present on the first occasion looked me hard in the eye several times and then came over to whisper: '*You* have to do it. No one else is capable. No one else even sees.'

On the first occasion, the correction went well. On the second, it didn't. Looking back, I can see the reason it didn't was because Leviathan knew exactly what I'd do—and had already called up spiritual reinforcements.

Many years later, I discovered that the seaside town where the summer mission was conducted was one of the top witchcraft hotspots of Australia. So, although I am not a natural leader, I was the right person to pull the team back when they'd trespassed into territory where the enemy could legally retaliate. It was a simple matter of not dishonouring God in worship.

As a general rule we don't realise how easy it is to slide into dishonour of God, even in the middle of prayer or praise, community or communion. It isn't honouring of others to remain silent when they have crossed the border from respect into disrespect. It is in fact putting them in harm's way—because most believers have no intention of dishonouring God. They do so ignorantly and inadvertently.

Yet that doesn't change Resheph's rights to retaliate against us. It will wait for the best opportunity to inflict reprisal—dishonour for dishonour—and, unless we repent, it will do so via our physical, mental or monetary welfare. Why does God allow this? Simply so we will be drawn back to Him.

Over a long period of time, I've come to realise why our world is in the grip of Resheph and why it has such strong influence in the economic sphere as well as in the health aspects of all our lives. It's said that, early in the twentieth century, *The Times* sent out an inquiry to famous authors of the era, asking the question, 'What's wrong with the world today?' They allegedly received this answer by reply post:

Dear Sir,

I am.

Yours, G.K. Chesterton.

There are moments when I see myself and I know a similar truth. *What's wrong with the world? I am.* There are times when I know myself inordinately beloved of the Father. Yet there are also times when I know that, like Isaiah, I am a woman of unclean lips and I live amongst a people of unclean lips. Every word from my mouth is tainted and I live in a society where every word is tainted. It is therefore impossible to truly honour God, until we ask Jesus our mediator to fix our words before any prayer ascends to the Father.

When the Israelites wandering in the wilderness dishonoured God as well as Moses, they were attacked by venomous serpents—'*nachash*'. So God told Moses to create a bronze serpent—'*seraph*'—and put it on a pole so people could look up and live. Resheph is a seraph and a bringer of both healing and burning fever. We can see it at work here, first retaliating for dishonour to God and then, at His gracious behest, healing those who looked to Him. The metal serpent, high and lifted up, was prophetic of Jesus. However about a millennium later, this treasured memento called 'Nehushtan' was kept in the Temple and had degenerated into an idol. King Hezekiah ordered its destruction.[121]

God had given the people an access point for blessing, but it had become an idol. Is this what has happened to our world today? As I am writing these words, a disease called COVID-19 has turned our entire planet upside down. Economies have gone into freefall as fear of a rampaging virus has caused unprecedented national responses to contain the spread of the disease. In my own country of Australia, this last half year has seen intense drought, widespread fire, financial ruin and a mental health crisis in addition to the health issues associated with coronavirus. All these hallmarks are symptomatic of the activity of Resheph. And this says to me: the root of the problem is dishonour of God in prayer.

This means the problem is us—believers. As GK Chesterton said about the problem: 'I am.'

Our methods of prayer have become our Nehushtan. What is meant as our access point to God has become, for so many of us, our idol.

As soon as I stepped over the threshold, my prayers changed in an unexpected way. I'd never before considered asking Jesus to amend my words, even to cancel what I'd asked for—if He thought fit. Suddenly it was a natural part of my approach to God. Suddenly I wanted Jesus to make my words holy and honouring.

Instinctively, I knew I didn't have a clue how to do it myself. My culture is so steeped in dishonour and discourtesy[122] that the only way I can hope to honour God is by asking Jesus, my mediator and advocate, to do it for me.

Jesus was very systematic in His approach to warfare with Leviathan-Resheph—but there was never any sense of formula about His strategies. Neither should we try to find a formula for any healing of history He calls us to participate in. Guidelines, yes—especially about honouring God and honouring each other—but prescriptive method, no.

Jesus was also comprehensive and economical in His approach to healing. When He healed a person, so often He was healing the land at the same time. At the dedication of the First Temple, God had promised Solomon:

> *If I close the sky so there is no rain, or if I command the locust to devour the land, or if I send a plague among My people, if My people, who are called by My name, will humble themselves and pray and seek My face and turn from their wicked ways, then I will hear from heaven, and I will forgive their sin and will heal their land.*
>
> 2 Chronicles 7:13–14 NIV

The word for *plague* here is Deber, the 'speaker' and companion of Resheph, the bringer of heat and drought. This promise of God is dense with allusion. An alternative word for *plague* comes from *striking a threshold* and *refusing covenant*—and therefore dishonouring God. Likewise, an alternative word for *locust swarm* is the same as that for *haughty* or *proud*. God is making clear that the precursor to healing the land is turning from pride and dishonour. It's becoming humble and therefore ceasing to defile God and others through arrogance or jealousy.

Holiness, honour and humility are all related in the life of Jesus. They came together to such a high degree that He was able to specialise in the simultaneous treating of several historical traumas at once. For example, when He met the woman at the well in Samaria, His conversation flows from subtle to forthright, offering the living water of healing in regard to:

- the long-standing ethnic rift between the Samaritans and the Jews
- the discrimination of Ezra and Nehemiah with regard to foreign wives—in their zeal for racial purity, they didn't offer them the choice of Ruth or Rahab
- the abuse of the foreigner Hagar who encountered the 'Living One' at a well

However, living water is required for the coronation of a king. So Jesus, in offering it, was proposing to heal the kingship:

- the first king *in* Israel, though not *of* Israel, was crowned at this spot. Abimelech, son of Gideon, killed all but one of his seventy brothers to eliminate all possible rivals.

- the arrogance of the fourth king *of* Israel, Rehoboam, resulted in the kingdom of David splitting into two parts at this place.

So when Jesus came to reunify the kingdom, these were the defilements of kingship He had to heal: pride and murder. Humility and love were needed to overcome these wounds of history. The scars went back, in fact, to the time of Jacob when Simeon and Levi avenged the rape of their sister Dinah by killing all the local inhabitants—even though Prince Shechem wanted to marry Dinah and to covenant with her family. As a consequence of their treaty violation, Simeon and Levi lost the favour of their father regarding their inheritance.

But there are spiritual aspects to the worship that need to be healed too.

- Shechem was known in the ancient world as having a temple to Baal Berith, *the 'lord of the covenant'*. Outside Israel, it was reputed to have a shrine to Resheph.

- This suggests a covenant with Death. It recalls stories of those who, like Ishtar, descended to the underworld, and were assaulted by plague demons, then had the reviving 'water of life' sprinkled on them.

Jesus effectively told those worshippers of Resheph in town that He is the true Water of Life. His visit to the Sychar-Shechem area was not the only time Jesus visited Samaria. After returning from the Mount of

Transfiguration, He and His disciples also went through there. During this trip, an incident occurred that is often thought to be the origin of the nickname Jesus gave to James and John: *sons of thunder*. Was Jesus actually referencing Job 5:7, about '*the sons of Resheph*' when He described these two Galilean fishermen that way?

No context is given in Mark 3:17 for this nickname but it's almost universally linked by commentators to Luke 9:54. In that passage, the brothers wanted to call down fire from heaven to destroy a Samaritan village which refused to offer Jesus hospitality because He was heading for Jerusalem. In effect, they said to Jesus: 'You've been dishonoured. Can we retaliate on Your behalf with a bucketload of hot coals tipped from a celestial altar?'

When Jesus sent out the seventy disciples in pairs just after this incident, He instructed them to simply wipe the dust from their feet as they left any village that did not accept them. Since 'wiping the dust from your feet' was a cultural metaphor for leaving resentment behind, Jesus was merely saying: 'Guys, forgive 'em'.

The Greek word for *fire* in this passage about heavenly retribution is also that for *lightning*. So it's quite reasonable to link this back to *sons of thunder*. But it's also possible to link it to Resheph. Since the mission to the Samaritans occurred after the Transfiguration, it was supposed to be a healing and gospel-proclaiming exercise, not the start of a war. Yet both healing and war were associated with Resheph.

When the disciples returned, thrilled to report that demons were submitting to them through the power of the name of Jesus, He announced:

> '*I saw Satan fall like lightning from heaven...*'
>
> Luke 10:18 NIV

Having mentioned *lightning* and the *satan* in the same phrase, was Jesus referencing Resheph? Or some other entity? Is it Python? Or Azazel? It might be subtle to us, but it probably wasn't two millennia ago. The 'satan' after all is simply a title meaning the adversary, the opponent, the arch-enemy. It doesn't really specify which specific antagonist. So, although we have got used to the traditional assumption that the 'satan' is the same enemy every time it's mentioned in Scripture, that doesn't automatically follow. Certainly every reference could be to the same being, but there's also the possibility that we are facing different enemies at different times.

Jesus' next words don't help clarify this issue; in fact, they add another possibility to the mix:

> '*I have given you authority to trample on snakes and scorpions and to overcome all the power of the enemy, nothing will harm you.*'
>
> Luke 10:18 NIV

The next verse makes it clear these are spiritual enemies rather than physical ones. The 'scorpion' is a symbol of Leviathan but 'snake' could refer to Python or to any fallen seraph, including Resheph or Ziz.

But trampling on these particular creatures could also be an allusion to Horus, the son of Osiris, who is shown in a well-known magical carving standing on two crocodiles while holding snakes in one hand and scorpions in the other. Also in his hands are a lion and a gazelle. The crocodiles, snakes and scorpions all symbolise Horus' arch-enemy, Set, while both the lion and the gazelle symbolise Resheph. The iconography declares that Horus is triumphant over Set-Resheph. However it should also remind us of Psalm 91:

> *'You will tread on the lion and cobra, the young lion and the serpent you will trample down.'*
>
> Psalm 91:13 NIV

The word for *cobra* in this verse is 'pethen', *python*; for *young lion* is 'kephir' which also means *village*; and for *serpent*, 'tannin', thus *sea monster*.

Look at the matches! After coming down from the Mount of Transfiguration where the <u>seventy</u> **young lions** had their abode, Jesus sent <u>seventy</u> of His disciples out to the **villages** of Samaria and Galilee. He had replaced the corrupt government of the nations, the seventy principalities, with His own representatives who were commissioned to declare the coming of the Kingdom. On the joyful return of those ambassadors, He spoke of their authority—an authority that, in his subtle reference to Horus, spoke of power over the lord of the underworld, Set-Resheph.

But more than that, Jesus indicated that He'd turned the tables on the Tempter who tested Him in the wilderness beyond Gilead. This was the threshold spirit who, after trying to convince Him to turn stones into bread (was He in Lo Debar, *no bread*, at the time?), quoted the previous two verses from Psalm 91 about angels lifting up those who love God so they do not even dash their foot against a stone. This word, *dash*, can also be *strike*, *smite*, *stumble*, *trample*. It is also related to the word for *plague* and to *refusal of covenant*.

If you are trampling on something—most especially a threshold stone—you are refusing covenant. So when Jesus spoke about trampling on snakes and scorpions, He was not just talking of triumph over the power of the enemy. He was talking about the power to annul ungodly covenants.

All of these references to the satan, lightning, snakes, scorpions and the power of the enemy suggest Resheph, Set and Horus, a trio of deities worshipped in Egypt. Is there any place in first century Israel where there was a history of Egyptian influence and devotion to these specific godlings? Of course there was.

Scythopolis, *city of the Scythians*, was the leading city of the Decapolis[123] and the only one situated on the western bank of the Jordan River. At some time in the two or three centuries before Christ, it appears to have been taken over and settled by Scythian archers—hence the name.[124] In some places, the more things change, the more they stay the same. This is one of them. Scythopolis had previously been known as Beit She'an, and originally been called Beth Shan—the fortress where Mekal-Resheph, the archer godling, was worshipped. This was the location where the bodies of Saul and his sons were displayed on the walls.

So, taking into consideration the past behaviour of Jesus when it came to selecting the location for a provocative announcement, I think it extremely likely that He said, '*I saw Satan fall like lightning from heaven,*' in the vicinity of Scythopolis—ancient Beth Shan.

Sometimes the darkness feels overwhelming. The interconnecting and overlapping links between these sinister spiritual entities become confusing and even contradictory after a while. And there's so many of them, who may or may not be the same spirit: Leviathan, Resheph, Osiris, Set, Nergal, Shamash, Mekal, Hadad, Rimmon, Moloch, Hercules Melqart... not to mention quite a few more I haven't highlighted yet.

In a very real sense we can bundle them all up and sweep them away and simply say: *Jesus overcome them all, every last one*. But in another sense, when we have a specific covenant coming down our bloodline with one of them, it is not sufficient to say: 'I renounce every last covenant with any of the spirits who claim rulership of the underworld.' Such a vague statement simply doesn't cut it in the intensely legalistic atmosphere of the spiritual realms. Spirits don't give up their legal rights so easily. They do not extend grace. Only God does that.

Sometimes it's necessary to know which spirit is attacking us in order to have some understanding of the spiritual rights they have. For example, if we can positively identify Leviathan, then we can know the issue is dishonour. If we can positively identify Pan or Azazel, we know the issue is rejection. If we can positively identify Ziz, then we know the issue involves complicity with forgetting truth.

As I was writing *Dealing with Leviathan*, I felt like a bit of a fraud. I've never experienced the severity of retaliation

I've seen visited on the lives of others. I knew nothing of the close-quarter combat many of my friends have experienced. So I was always writing from the outside, looking in. However, when I came across references to Resheph and learned of the symbolism attached to it, I was no longer viewing the situation from a distance. Where I felt I could recognise a few minor brush-bys of Leviathan in my life, it was totally different with Resheph. I could see it writ large from a very early age.

It would have been possible for me, had I never found Resheph, to simply say: *because honour has been so important to me, I've avoided a great deal of Leviathan's backlash. Sure honour was in danger of becoming an idol in my life, but God in His grace made me aware of that. So, as long as He continues to help me to keep honour properly balanced, Leviathan should not be able to affect my life in a major way.*

I could have said that but it would have been extreme naïvety. Leviathan was indeed there, masked as Resheph. It took a long while for me to accept that Leviathan and Resheph as the same entity, even though I suspected it from the start. The major obstacle in this regard was the very different iconography that appeared to separate the two. The symbols were so dissimilar: Leviathan was imaged as a dragon, a crocodile or a scorpion. Resheph on the other hand was pictured as lightning, an archer, a stag, burning coals.

But finally I realised my thinking was locked in by western cultural boundaries. Just as I'd had a problem with connecting death and honour, so now my problem was animals. I could see that a dragon, a crocodile and a scorpion all had stinging, lashing tails, therefore it was ok in my mind to class them together—but a stag simply did not fit in this rigid category system. So as far as I was concerned, that initially cast excessive doubt on the possibility that Resheph and Leviathan were different names for the same spirit.

It was only when I discovered that Nergal—a deity widely recognised as the Mesopotamian alter-ego of Resheph—was symbolised by a lion, a gazelle and a vulture[125] that I rethought my position. These emblems so defied categorisation my objections crumbled. The reasons to doubt the equivalence of Leviathan and Resheph were gone and I was left with the numerous attributes they have in common (LISTED IN APPENDIX 2).

Throughout this process—the long years of discovery about the tactics of Python and Ziz, Leviathan and Lilith, Azazel and Belial, as well as Rachab—I've learned that, if we want to deal in a practical way with specific spiritual issues in our lives, it's a good thing to be able to identify the problem and what—or who—is behind it. It's not good enough to apply a Scriptural verse about healing as a band-aid to the cancer of unforgiveness. The blood of Jesus is not magic medicine: the power of the Cross is designed to work in combination with genuine repentance to affect miraculous and life-changing transformations. However, as wise spiritual surgeons, we need to know what the real problem is. It is God's complete prerogative to choose to heal sovereignly, but most of the time He expects us to meet the preconditions and repent—before He allows His grace to kick in. Otherwise, the disease will quickly return. And what's the point of that when He wants us to experience shalom, *wholeness* and *health*, not an unremitting cycle of disease?

The Fruit of the Spirit that is an effective weapon against Leviathan is peace. Dishonour leads to the absence of *shalom* in our lives and thus to an inability to inherit the promises of God with regard to well-being, welfare, prosperity, soundness, integrity, completeness and recompense. The importance of honour is the major theme of the previous book in this series.

Putting this another way, the absence of shalom invites the presence of disease and dispossession, deficiency and deprivation. These factors point more to Resheph the plague-bringer or its counterpart Melqart, who claims rights to money management in our lives. Plague is indicative, throughout Scripture, of a withdrawal of God's protection because of covenant violation or because of a refusal to break off ungodly covenants.

Because the essential nature of covenant is oneness—and this is the critical aspect that differentiates it from contract—there are much greater ramifications to covenant breach than mere legal infringements. We tear asunder our relationship with Jesus, we spit in His face, we pull at His beard, we take the whip to His back and then we say: 'But where were You when I needed Your help?'

We believe we have the authority to treat snakes and scorpions like Leviathan-Resheph just as we please when, in fact, we've totally misunderstood the nature of authority. It is a delegated power to *uphold* God's Word; we have not had conferred on us the right to make up our own rules when it comes to these fallen powers.

Authority and permission are not exactly the same thing. We may not have authority to deal with a particular spiritual issue, but God may in fact grant us permission at times in specific cases. Jesus, after all, had the authority to call on twelve legions of angels but He didn't have permission. We therefore need to stay within the boundaries of what He has granted. I learned this the hard way.

Back in *Dealing with Leviathan*, I described going to the Faroe Islands to see a total solar eclipse and, as a consequence, learning about the lines in the landscape Leviathan uses for its own purposes. The line of totality of an eclipse is not dissimilar in many respects to a ley line.

On the way back from the Faroes, I got off the ship in Newcastle-on-Tyne and finally did something that God had been instructing me to do for years: *go to Hadrian's Wall and turn right.* I'd been saying to Him every time He told me, 'Hadrian's Wall is quite long. Is there any particular place You'd like me to turn right?' and it had taken me well over a decade to discover the turning-point He had in mind.

Because I live in Australia, the opportunity to get to Hadrian's Wall doesn't arise all that often—but I'd made a couple of attempts. Back in 1998, I'd got close. The car I was driving broke down not far from the Wall and I'd spent the day with my friend Linda in the pub at Stagshaw Roundabout while waiting for the AA to arrive and tow the vehicle to Newcastle. I've dined out on the story several times. I'd rung the AA from the phone in the pub but my Australian accent was too much for the receptionist who couldn't make any sense of the location I was giving him for the site of the breakdown.

In desperation, I asked the waitress to explain to him that it was just up the road, a few hundred metres from the Errington Arms. 'Eets a' Stigshoer Roondoboot,' she kept repeating in her strong Geordie accent. After five minutes or so, the receptionist gave up. 'Put the Australian back on,' I heard him say. 'I've got a better chance with her.'

As I finally sat down with my friend to make an order for a counter lunch, I did a lot of praying that I'd actually been understood on the other end of the line. The waitress took my drink order. 'Do you do lemon, lime and bitters?' I asked, mentioning a well-known non-alcoholic cocktail in Australia.

She looked at me strangely before nodding. 'Are yee sure?'

'It's common in Australia,' I said.

'Wi can dee tha,' she said. But the look she gave me as she went showed how dubious she was.

When the drink arrived, it didn't look normal. Instead of the pale pink of a few drops of angostura bitters with crushed lemon and lime, ice and soda, it looked like the entire bottle of the aromatic tonic had been poured in. 'I don't think that's your average LLB,' Linda said, peering at the traditional lime and lemon slices on the rim. 'I think they've gone a bit overboard on the bitters. Maybe you should send it back.'

But I felt a lot beholden to the waitress for her efforts on the phone. So I squeezed in some lime and took a tentative sip. 'It tastes a bit odd...' I paused. 'It's not undrinkable.' I took another sip.

'Don't look now,' Linda said, 'but the entire pub is watching you. I don't know what you're drinking but I think there are a couple of bets on as to whether you're going to make it through.'

I got halfway down the glass before people stopped watching, convinced I really was intending to drink the lot. By which time it had occurred to me that I had done something unspeakable to a half pint of Guinness.

So I had pretty memorable memories of *not* getting to Hadrian's Wall the first time. The second occasion, a few years later, I simply got lost. Nothing as unforgettable as that day in the Errington Arms—which, the mishap with the drinks aside, was a time of fervent prayer for the car and of desperately hoping the AA man understood where it was broken down.

Over sixteen years went by before I discovered how badly I failed the test the Lord had set that day. And I discovered this not long after I'd been to a workshop on the Courts of Heaven. There I'd been encouraged to try the protocols for myself. 'Don't worry about making mistakes,' the coordinator said. 'There's a lot of grace when you first start.'

But not knowing where to start, I decided to ask the Lord what I should take to the Courts. 'What do You think I should ask for?' I said to Him.

His answer was a total surprise. He suggested that I ask for 'walls' for a friend of mine. So I told her what I felt God had said and asked her permission to go to the Courts on her behalf. She said yes, particularly because of a new residential venture she was about to embark on that involved the concept of being 'without walls'. However, as soon as others found out about this proposed appeal to heaven, they too wanted in—none of them felt they had appropriate boundaries in their lives. Half a dozen people eventually put their hands up to be involved in a joint petition, a 'class action' as it were, to the Courts of Heaven. We based the wording of the appeal on the model in *The Cosmic Hierarchy* by Tom Hawkins and we prayed over it, making adjustments and refinements over a period of several weeks. Then on the same day, at the same time, in our various locations across two different countries, we read our petition together—asking for an answer in 52 days. After all, that's how long Nehemiah took to build the walls of Jerusalem, so it appeared to be an appropriate timeframe to receive God's ruling on the matter.

As the time approached and the 52 days were almost up, I went to God and asked Him if He were ready to deliver judgment. 'Your request will be granted,' He said.

I smiled with relief. I would be able to report success to everyone in the group.

'However...' God went on. 'There has been a counter-petition which I have also granted.'

'*Counter*-petition?' I asked, stunned. No one had ever warned me that was even a remote possibility.

'There has been a request for doubling. That you not get one set of walls but two.'

I took a deep breath. Suddenly 'appropriate boundaries' had turned into a trap. Should I go back to the Courts and ask for an injunction against this second set of walls? *But wait...* 'Excuse me, Lord, for asking—but *why* would You grant this? You must have a good reason.'

'Tell Me: what does it mean to you to be "between the walls"?'

What instantly came to mind was the Antonine Wall in lowland Scotland, Hadrian's Wall in northern England and 'the Borders' between them. That was the location of the ancient Roman province of Valentia and there, too, some historians think is the original 'Avalon' of Arthurian fame. Which probably means 'Valhalla' is there too.

Valentia — Avalon — Valhalla. I put one 'val' and another 'val' and yet another 'val' together and came up with a very unpleasant possibility. 'Is "between the walls" the same as the "valley of the shadow of death"?' I asked God.

'There's a symbolic equivalence. On your way back from the Faroe Islands, I want you to go to Hadrian's Wall and turn right. There is something I want you to do there but I want you to be safe. No spirit can challenge your legal right to be "between the walls" when they are the ones who have asked for you to be placed there.'

'That's great,' I said. But I didn't feel great at all. I've only ever been to the Courts of Heaven this once and I hope you now understand why. I'm really reluctant to be subject to counter-petitions that are both unexpected and have inbuilt unknowns.

Now of course the problem with going to Hadrian's Wall and turning right was that it was still as long as ever and finding the spot to turn right was still as problematic as ever. But I applied myself to scouring ancient documents and old maps with renewed vigour and finally discovered sufficient information about the pre-Roman roads to be able to look up Google Earth. I could even find street view so I'd know exactly what I was looking for when I got there... and, as I checked it out, I said to myself: *I've been there. I know this place.* I told myself it was impossible but everything looked so very familiar, I brought up all the landscape markers. 'Stagshaw Bank', it said. And there too was the Errington Arms, marked so clearly on the map.

'What?!' I said to God. 'How can this be? I've been looking for this spot for... well, it seems like forever... and I knew where it was all the time? Why didn't You tell me?'

'You were supposed to pray *for the place*, not for the car,' He said. 'That's why it broke down there.'

I suddenly realised God had put a test in front of me and I'd failed miserably. 'If I'd known it was a test, I'd have done differently,' I said. 'Not that I'm excusing myself. But next time there's a test, can You give me a hint in advance?'

Time went by. I went to the Faroes, came back, went to Hadrian's Wall and turned right and stayed 'between the walls' for most of three weeks. Because of what I'd learned about the connection between Leviathan and lines in the landscape, I tried diligently to avoid ley lines—on the principle that this would avoid Leviathan. But, as God laid out the path before me, this strategy of evasion was singularly unsuccessful.

I did in fact find a hill that probably isn't the real 'Avalon' but has all the right symbolism anyway and I managed to be the first person there over Easter as the post-winter season opened. The guide was only too happy to give me a personal tour and let me explore privately. So I had extensive opportunity to pray there in peace.

One thing I came to realise during this time—"between the walls" was a safety zone. Outside the walls was not. In fact, I learned some very important lessons on the difference between *permission* and *authority* on venturing outside the walls.

Back in 2001, during the time of my second abortive trip to find Hadrian's Wall when I'd got lost, I'd been keen while I was in England to find a particular carving I'd once seen in a photograph. I had a sense the symbolism had something to do with my family and that the spiritual implications were not good. Problem was: I had no idea where the carving was. The photo didn't say. But it was somewhere in England—I presumed in a museum or gallery. Finding that needle in the haystack would be beyond miraculous but I prayed fervently for God to lead me to the place where this carving was. Eventually I returned home to Australia without ever coming across it. Still I wasn't disappointed because I knew it had been a long shot at best.

But in 2007, six years later, I was to become acutely upset. Because, by that time, Google had become a formidable search engine, and I discovered the location of the carving. It was in a church in a small market town in northern England. The *exact* town I'd chosen to visit for two days. I could actually remember getting to the gate of the church just as the sky started to drizzle. I vividly recalled deciding not to go in but to return to the warmth of the B&B and come back in the morning. But the next day circumstances changed and I never did go to explore the church.

Three things I realised: first, against staggering odds, God had indeed answered my prayer and had led me to the exact place where the carving was. (Wow! How often in life do we turn aside on the threshold and not realise it?) Secondly, I hadn't asked to see the carving, just to go to where it was. (Should I have been more specific?) Thirdly, having got there, it had been my choice to make comfort my priority: I hadn't actually asked God if I should go in or not. (Memo to self: talk to God more.)

So, as I made my plans in 2015, it occurred to me that staying in the Borders presented an opportunity to redress my tragic mistake and actually see the carving and pray over it. Sure the church where it was situated was outside the walls, but still it was only four hours away. The day was beautiful and the traffic easy. I found the church, parked the car, opened the door and was slammed on the head by a ball of slurried ice. The sky had darkened abruptly and sleet was pelting down. 'I was stopped by drizzle last time,' I said to myself. 'Am I going to be hindered by this?' I grabbed a raincoat. 'No!' A harder iceball hit me on the head. And then another.

I took the hint and got back into the car. This was a very odd storm. Slowly and carefully, I drove back out of town, just to find out if my suspicions were correct. Yes, it was incredibly localised. Just beyond the town the sky was blue and the day was sunny and bright. I drove right around the town, checking on all sides, and half an hour later got back to the church. The weather seemed to have settled right down. I opened the door and got slammed by another two iceballs.

I drove off. 'This is not an attack, is it?' I said to God when I got calm enough. 'This is not the enemy. At least it might be the enemy, but You're allowing it because it's really a message from You. What are You telling me?'

'You don't have authority there,' He said.

'I know that,' I said. 'But I've been praying about this for years.'

'You don't have My permission either,' He went on. 'And I'm not going to give it to you if you ask. This is a matter for the people of the church to deal with. You are not to interfere or usurp their authority.'

I felt very small at that moment. I'd come half-way across a planet and I was unlikely ever to return to this town. 'What do I have permission to do?' I asked. 'Can I pray anything at all?'

'It's a *church*,' God said, as if that explained everything.

'Huh?'

'You have permission to be part of their communion. You have permission to join them in worship.'

So I did. I came back the following Sunday. And I resisted the temptation to pray about the carving because I knew I didn't have authority and I knew I wasn't going to get permission. Much later, I realised this was a test. It was a trial to find out if I'd obey God when He said 'no' to something I'd invested a lot of time and prayer as well as emotional and spiritual energy in. I messed up the test at Stagshaw Roundabout back in 1998, and I had to redo it. However I still had to learn that, just because God has called you to pray about something, doesn't mean you should assume you have greater authority than you do. He retains the rights to delegate or withhold permission as He sees fit. Jesus had the authority to call on twelve legions of angels but He didn't have permission.

And importantly, from what God had said right from the beginning, 'between the walls' the legal rights He had granted me could not be challenged. But outside the walls, it was a different matter. And the church was very definitely *outside* the walls.

When travelling through the 'valley of the shadow of death'—whether it's a physical or spiritual landscape—every step needs to be guided by Jesus. After seventeen days in lowland Scotland, I finally got enough feel for the land to be able to say: 'All I've been hearing about ever since I got here is hundreds of armies criss-crossing the land. But it's deeper than that. This landscape *breeds* armies.'

It felt right. After all, out of this landscape had come the word 'bereaved'—originally meaning that 'we've been visited by the Reivers.' I immediately checked on the oldest recorded name for that region of the Borders. It dated from Roman times and was a tribal designation: the land of the Gadeni, *men of battle*.

Yes, that kind of name would do it. A land that breed armies. But Gadeni, *men of battle*, reminded me of one of the sons of Jacob—Gad, the patriarch whose name means *troop* or *fortune*. It also reminded me of the territory his descendants occupied as part of the tribal confederation: the land of the Gadarenes, the location where Jesus met the man afflicted by the demonic 'Legion'.

In case you haven't guessed it, we're back in Gilead—a land which, like the Borders of Scotland, was the buffer zone between the Roman Empire and barbarian tribes. And at least on the *northern* frontier, there was a line: Hadrian's Wall. Allegedly for defensive purposes, but history shows it was almost as porous as a sieve. My belief is that it is religious in nature.

Hadrian, the emperor who razed Jerusalem to the ground, renamed the city and made a point of defiling both Jewish and Christian sacred sites, was a follower of Pythagoras. His building programme throughout the empire highlights his beliefs. Now, as I've pointed out in *Dealing with Leviathan*, Pythagoras is not simply an ancient mathematician; he was the founder of a religion involving numbers that was, and remains, the greatest opponent of Christianity across the ages. That statement probably seems like a massive exaggeration; however, the war conducted by the early Christian writers against Pythagorean theurgy is, like the war Jesus conducted against Resheph, openly on display in the gospels and epistles.[126]

The positioning of Hadrian's Wall indicates to me that, while it had many different cultic sites along its length, overall it was dedicated to Python Apollo. It has a latitude of around 55° which, while not an exact golden ratio of the equator to the pole, is a close practical approximation, especially since a wall at the perfect spot would be nearly twice the length.[127]

The whole point of building a boundary line for Apollo, *the sun god*, is subtle self-adulation. Hadrian's family name was Aelia, for Helios, *the sun*. After destroying Jerusalem, he renamed it 'Aelia Capitolina' and forbade, on pain of death, any Jew to set foot inside it. This interdiction remained in place until the time of Constantine who brought back the name Jerusalem.[128] Hadrian defiled both Jewish and Christian sites—building a temple to Jupiter on the site of the Second Temple, and positioning a statue of himself on a horse where the Holies of Holies had been. He also erected a temple to Venus on the site of the resurrection and a shrine to Tammuz in the cave in Bethlehem where Jesus was born.

When we rename things, as Hadrian did to Jerusalem after 136 A.D., an ungodly covenant layer is created. It's sub-surface poison. And time does not dissipate it.

When I was teaching mathematics, I always tried to avoid the golden ratio. I was persuaded for many years that, because it was integral to the pentagram, then it was a satanic symbol. Perhaps too—as so many people were wont to claim—it was an emblem of the goddess. God really had to whack my thinking dozens of times before I got the message that it was nothing of the kind.

He'd ask me sternly as I would cut a papaya in half and notice the five-pointed star inside: 'So who do you think created this? The goddess?' Or I'd throw some the blue star-petals of borage into lemonade and He'd demand: 'I suppose the goddess was responsible for this design, right?' And then, when I'd picked up a tiny ram's horn shell from a sandy beach, He'd pressure me for an answer to another of these same rhetorical questions. He was relentless.

Everywhere I looked, the golden ratio was screaming out for attention and God was insisting on His rights as creator. At last, I surrendered and took a long and serious look at its mathematics as well as its history. And I reached the conclusion, after a great deal of investigation, that everything in creation bears this special mark—and it is God's mathematical signature. You'll find it three times encoded in Genesis 1:1 so, to say that it is demonic in origin or a symbol of the goddess, is to agree that the satan has a claim on it. It's to say the enemy has legitimate rights to what's been stolen from God.

It's to dishonour the true Creator.

Dealing with Leviathan looks at the fervent desire within many cultures to appropriate Zion—to transplant Jerusalem so that, when Jesus returns, He'll touchdown in some other country. But now we're looking at the opposite: the aspiration to claim the sacred places for the burning sun and for death.[129] These are the holy spaces that rightly belong to Jesus, 'the Sun of righteousness' who arose with healing in His wings.

Hercules Melqart tried to take the Temple precincts; Helios or Apollo set up camp in Aelia Capitolina; Mithras, 'the Invincible Sun' occupied along with the Roman legions; Ra with the Egyptians. And Resheph, the killing heat of the sun and a healer as well as a destroyer is—like them—the counterfeit of the Sun of righteousness.

> *'The day is coming, burning like a furnace, when all the arrogant and every evildoer will be stubble; the day is coming when I will set them ablaze,' says the Lord of Hosts. 'Not a root or branch will be left to them. But for you who fear My name, the Sun of righteousness will rise with healing in its wings, and you will go out and leap like calves from the stall.'*
>
> Malachi 4:1–2 BSB

With healing in His wings: that was why the people seeking help from Jesus all wanted to touch the 'hem' of His garment. The ends of a Jewish prayer shawl were called 'wings' and the fringe 'feathers'. The prophecy of Malachi was about a Messiah who could heal everyone through mediatory prayers to the Father. So people coming to Jesus wanted to attach themselves to His prayer life and they did that by touching the 'hem' of His garment.

It's still true. Our prayers avail nothing. It's only as we attach ourselves to the prayer life of Jesus as He mediates on our behalf before the throne of God that we bring healing down to earth.

Jesus calls us to heal people in His name, but also the land in His name. Leviathan creates lines and paths in the landscape as routes of both access and escape. Resheph, utilising Saul's covenant with the underworld, was able to defile an ancient trading route. It's no coincidence that Resheph's Phoenician counterpart is Melqart, *the king of the city of the underworld*, whose twin pillars of religion were money through trade and death through fire.[130]

Both these pillars can be summarised as: *insatiable consumption*. And *consume* is an alternative meaning for Resheph.[131] That reflects the ancient notion of Sheol, the realm of the dead, as a place that can never be satisfied; it is all-consuming; no matter how many souls it gets, it wants more; no matter how much 'stuff' it gets, it wants more.

Here too we can bring together the notion of fire with its ravenous need for more fuel, the unquenchable flames of jealousy and even Resheph's relationship to mental illness. Perhaps there is no better illustration of this combination than is outlined in the story of the Babylonian monarch, Nebuchadnezzar. The themes of desire, jealousy, fire and insanity are all there as he moves from a rapacious desire for all-encompassing worship to the episode of the fiery furnace before finally descending into madness.

The Russian philosopher, Nikolai Berdyaev, sums up the issue of consumption:

> *There are two symbols, bread and money;*
> *and there are two mysteries,*
> *the eucharistic mystery of bread*
> *and the satanic mystery of money.*
> *We are faced with the great task:*
> *to overcome the rule of money and*
> *to establish in its place the rule of bread.*

Bethlehem, *house of bread*, is also *house of war*. The Hebrew language recognised *bread* and *war* as related because warfare consumes, just as Sheol consumes, just as jealousy consumes.

But Jesus, the one born in Bethlehem, came to establish the rule of shared bread. And the war He conducted was against the young lions, the principalities of the nations, who had brought destruction to the land as well as the people. He walked the same trading path, trekking along the very same route that Saul's bones had followed. The trail led inexorably to the outskirts of Jerusalem. Later He went into the Temple to expel the traders in shekels from Tyre, just as God had once cast out the spirit known as the 'Prince of Tyre' from heaven itself.

To demonstrate that His actions had wrought healing in

the nation, He brought Lazarus back to life. He'd brought many others back before—but previously all had been on the same day. Perhaps some of His disciples thought He was resuscitating, rather than raising from the dead. But by waiting until the fourth day, there could be no doubt any longer of His conquest of the underworld.

And since He has accomplished this great victory, what does He want us to bring back to life, by attaching ourselves to the hem of His garment? How does He want us to spread the shalom He has brought into the world through this triumph over death?

Prayer

It is vitally important to recognise that prayer is about relationship with the Father. None of the prayers in this book are intended as a formula but as a guideline to help you realign yourself with the holy Trinity. They are meant as a starting point for a conversation.

Transformation is only possible as you hold onto the hem of Jesus' prayer shawl and ask Him to mediate before the Father for you. In the end, it's all about Him!

Abba, You said to the sea, 'Thus far you shall come, but no farther; and here shall your proud waves stop.' And likewise, You said to me, 'Thus far you shall come, but no farther; and here shall your pride stop.' But I stepped over the line.

You created me in love and for love and, because of Your love, You set boundaries in place: 'No farther,' You said. But I stepped over the line. I stepped out of holiness into sin—I exchanged truth for a lie and Your glory for dishonour.

You said, '*I am the Creator. Worship of My creation is off limits.*' You also said, '*I will give you all the gifts you need. Everyone else's stuff is off limits.*' You also said, '*I will give you your daily bread. Worship of money is off limits.*'

'*Thus far you shall come, but no farther.*'

Your Word is no longer considered important. Instead of a gold-standard, it's been updated to reflect our desire to exploit, to consume, to devour, to step over the line. We have called evil good and good evil. We've used and abused people and land, law and business—even love itself. We've covenanted with angelic majesties like Resheph-Leviathan and because they're mighty cosmic beings, we've felt enlarged and sensed the expansion of our spirits—and so we thought it was You. We didn't look at the fruit.

Forgive me, Abba, for crossing ungodly thresholds I was never meant to cross. Forgive me, Abba, for not crossing the holy threshold into my calling—or for crossing it wrapped in the grave-clothes of dishonour.

Teach me to choose respect to produce love.

Teach me to choose gratitude to produce joy.

Teach me to choose integrity to produce peace.

Teach me to choose You, Jesus.

In Your Name. Amen.

7

The Deer at the Dawn of the Day

Having disarmed principalities and powers, He made a public spectacle of them, triumphing over them.

Colossians 2:15 NKJV

Thanks be to God, who in Christ always leads us in triumphal procession, and through us spreads the fragrance of the knowledge of Him everywhere.

2 Corinthians 2:14 ESV

I USED TO THINK THESE VERSES were metaphorical and that Paul was merely using the images of Roman political life to make a point about how comprehensive Jesus' victory was. After all, he uses the technical term, 'triumph', not 'ovation'. A 'triumph' was the highest honour possible, while an 'ovation' was a lesser award.

Warrior kings and peoples, on their defeat, would be marched in chains through the streets of Rome, humiliated and disgraced, forced to kneel before the emperor's throne and then, more often than not, executed. Flower petals were often strewn in the victorious general's path and fragrant incense was burned along the route of the triumphal procession. This is what Paul is referring to when he speaks of *'the fragrance of the knowledge of Him.'*

And that aroma is literal, it's not symbolic. When it comes to Jesus' victory over Resheph, the idea that Paul was speaking metaphorically no longer rings true for me. The aroma is myrrh: standing for *remembrance*.[132]

And that aroma absolutely drenched the garden outside the tomb where Jesus was laid. The fragrance of myrrh would have wafted through on every whispering breeze. That's because Nicodemus had brought a hundred *litra* of myrrh and aloes to the tomb. Now we might not have any real grid of experience to judge that quantity of oil. However we should be able to tell it's a staggering amount by noting the severity of the criticism levelled at Mary Magdalene. Just a few days previously she had been condemned for expending just one single *litra* when she anointed Jesus during a supper at Bethany.

Nicodemus and the women who brought spices to the tomb helped fulfil an extraordinary prophecy: they created the 'mountain of spices' mentioned in the very last verse of the Song of Songs.

> *'O you who sit in the gardens,*
> *My companions are listening for your voice—*
> *Let me hear it!'*
>
> *'Hurry, my beloved,*
> *And be like a gazelle or a young stag*
> *On the mountains of spices.'*

Song of Songs 8:13-14 NASB

These words are just seven verses beyond the mention of 'resheph' and 'Sheol'—the burning coals of jealousy along with the Hebrew name for the underworld. They specifically refer to iconic symbols of the pagan deity Resheph—to gardens, to gazelles and stags. In addition, the words playfully hint of armies and of honour, as well as of David and his Lord.

Hebrew words are multi-faceted. In Western culture, we expect finely honed clarity. But this is a language of poetry and inscrutable mystery. Just as 'young stag' could point to a range of *strong leaders* including the morning star dubbed the 'deer of the dawn', so *gazelle*, 'tsebi', encodes a multiplicity of other possibilities too. It is identical to a word for *beauty*, *glory* and *honour*. It is also related to the word for *multi-coloured* or *variegated*—a concept that came to be associated with *grace*. André LaCocque points out the subtle allusions to God in the Song's repeated use of the word *gazelles* that an ancient listener would have immediately picked up: 'YHWH tseba'ôt [*Lord of hosts*] has become tseba'ôt [*gazelles*]; whilst El Shadday [*God Almighty*] has been changed into 'ayelôt hassadeh[*hinds of the field*].'

In addition, as already pointed out, the word translated as *stag*[133] is basically *strong leader*. So this exhortation of the Bride in the last verse of the Song poetically urges the Bridegroom to be a mighty champion, first in battle, and full of grace and honour. Prophetically, her encouragement foreshadows the joy of Resurrection Day.

In the garden, Mary Magdalene says to Jesus, '*They have taken my Lord away, and I don't know where they have put Him.*' Failing to recognise Him and assuming He is the gardener, she makes this statement, thereby echoing the same sentiment as that found in the wedding scene in the Song of Songs. The friends of the Bride ask:

> *'Where has your beloved gone, O most beautiful among women? Where has your beloved turned, that we may seek Him with you?'*
>
> Song of Songs 6:1 ESV

On the Cross, the last word Jesus spoke was, in Aramaic, 'kallah'—the cry of the Bridegroom. Nicodemus, recognising its significance, arranged for myrrh, oil of joy, to be brought to the tomb. He understood the implication of the spirit-blood and water flowing from the side of Jesus as the 'new birth' and realised that, just as Adam's bride, Eve, had been born from under his heart, so the Bride of the Second Adam would be born—by faith—in the same way. And so the story of the Bride of Christ begins in the garden outside the myrrh-saturated tomb where Jesus met her first representative: Mary Magdalene.

Mary's words not only contain lingering echoes of the wedding scene from the Song of Songs, but also remind us of the tragedy of Adam's bride. After the Fall, God the gardener came looking for mankind, saying: 'Where are you?' But, in this reversal of Eden, a representative of mankind comes looking for God, whom she mistakes for a gardener, asking: 'Where is He?'

Perhaps we should not be surprised at her identity, because her name was—astonishingly—prophesied in the last scene of the Song of Songs, just three verses before the mention of the *garden* and the *gazelle*. Magdalene comes from 'migdol', *a tower*, referred to in both verses 9 and 10.

Jesus was not only rehearsing the Marriage of the Lamb in the garden, and not only reversing Eden, but He was also despoiling pagan religion. Resheph was symbolised as a *stag* and titled *lord of the garden*. In the garden, Jesus showed Himself the *strong leader*, the Firstborn from the Dead and the true Lord of the Garden.

But that's not all. Besides being the *doorkeeper of the underworld*, Resheph was also called *doorwarden of the sun*—probably a reference to the *evening star*. And, as identical to the *morning star*, it is in Hebrew understanding *the deer that heralds the dawn*. Jesus, the 'Bright and Morning Star', burst through the doors of the underworld at daybreak as an angel-orchestrated earthquake broke open the tomb.

Once we recognise the ancient melody of Song of Songs playing in the background of the encounter between Jesus the Bridegroom, and Mary Magdalene representing the Bride of Christ, we can see how detailed the outworking of the prophecy was. And this remains true, despite the serious limitations in our knowledge about the religious rites associated with Resheph. The deer godling was exposed as a counterfeit and the true Lord of Healing had appeared.

The dialogue between Jesus and Mary in the garden is so simple it seems impossible that it should encode as much as it does. Within it is the report of a sweeping blitzkrieg conducted on multiple battle fronts. This single understated conversation indicates how many of God's arch-enemies have been utterly eliminated.

The reason I think we can speak of comprehensive and total defeat is because Resheph isn't the only deity Jesus took on during His harrowing of hell. There were many lordlings and godlings of the underworld, but there is one particular deity He devoted considerable attention to—ensuring that the war of total annihilation left nothing unturned. This deity was one I've mentioned only briefly in passing: Baal Hadad. Now Resheph and Baal Hadad are paired up in some Canaanite inscriptions, sometimes partners, sometimes apparently identical; and it was natural they should be associated since Baal Hadad was in charge of storms and Resheph of lightning and thunder.[134]

Baal Hadad was called *the cloud-rider*. That was a claim Jesus could not leave unchallenged. He began His campaign against Baal Hadad during His trial before the Sanhedrin. None of the witnesses could agree about what Jesus had said in His teaching, so Caiaphas had asked Him directly: 'Are you the Messiah?'

> *'I am,' said Jesus. 'And you will see the Son of Man sitting at the right hand of the Mighty One and coming on the clouds of heaven.'*

>   Mark 14:61–62 NIV

It was in fact this very claim to be 'the Cloud-Rider' at God's right hand that led directly led to His death. Caiaphas, apparently jubilant at Jesus' admission, immediately proclaimed there was no further need of witnesses. Jesus had condemned Himself out of His own mouth by quoting the vision of the prophet Daniel:

> *'Behold, with the clouds of heaven there came one like a son of man, and He came to the Ancient of Days and was presented before Him. And to Him was given dominion and glory and a kingdom, that all peoples, nations, and languages should*

> *serve Him; His dominion is an everlasting dominion, which shall not pass away, and His kingdom one that shall not be destroyed.'*
>
> Daniel 7:13–14 ESV

As Michael Heiser has pointed out, in the first century this prophecy about the Cloud-Rider was understood as referring to One who was co-regent with Yahweh. Baal Hadad, the 'Rider in the Clouds'[135] and the Storm-bringer, also claimed to be co-regent with the chief Canaanite deity.

Now we know a fair bit more about the liturgies associated with Baal Hadad than we do for any rites connected with Resheph.[136] At the end of each winter, the worshippers of Baal Hadad would stand outside a sacred cave and summon him forth from his imprisonment in the underworld. They would call out the ritual question: 'Where is the prince?' or 'Where is the lord?'

That question is, in fact, encoded in a name. A very famous name: Jezebel. *'Where is the lord?'* is what the name of this Phoenician princess means, and it comes from an annual ceremony to release Baal from the underworld. This shouldn't be a surprise once we realise her father was a priest of Baal.

Way back in the time of Elijah, the contest with the prophets of Baal on Mount Carmel was a battle with the worshippers of the Storm-bringer. For over three years, the skies had been shut up—and only when the people turned back to Yahweh did the rain return. Here Elijah foreshadows the triumph of Jesus over Baal Hadad— once again in the garden.

Let's go back to that deceptively simple question of Mary Magdalene. Basically her inquiry to the man she thinks is the gardener is just: *Where is the Lord?* She was outside a cave, a tomb—an entrance to the underworld—and her question is full of redolent echoes of pagan rites and of the infamous name, Jezebel. Those rites were tipped upside down and Mary shows us what Jezebel, Queen of Samaria, would look like, if she had ever been redeemed.[137]

So as well as Eden reversed and the Marriage of the Lamb rehearsed, there was vast despoiling of pagan religion going on as well. The name 'Baal' means *lord, master, husband*. Jesus effectively appropriated not just the sacred history of Baal but his mythic titles as well. In effect He said that nothing whatsoever belonged to Baal—not his legend, not his liturgy, not his titles, not his ceremonies, not his rituals, not even his name.

Jesus defeated Baal Hadad in a war of 'herem': one devoted to total destruction. Jesus just took everything apart. And He must have done the same to Resheph-Leviathan.

Yet, despite that, when we've been attacked by Resheph-Leviathan and we feel like we've been used for target practice by an entire battalion of archers,[138] it's all too easy to think, 'God, why have You forsaken me?' That of course is exactly what Jesus said on the Cross. It's the beginning of Psalm 22, the one that's headed up with words about *the deer at the dawn of the day*. But let us not only remember the beginning of that psalm but also its finale: '*He has accomplished it.*'

And He wants us, in relationship with Him, to work together to make manifest in the earth what He has already accomplished. He wants us to restore and revive, raise up and renew, reward and regenerate each other in Him to bring in His shalom.

In the final analysis, what convinced me that Resheph and Leviathan are one and the same is that the same Fruit of the Spirit overcomes them. Shalom, *peace* and *recompense*, overcomes Leviathan; while shalom, *soundness, health and prosperity*, overcome Resheph. Soundness and health overcome its tactic of sickness and disease; peace overcomes its tactic of war; and prosperity overcomes its tactic of instilling an obsessive desire for ever-increasing wealth. And if prosperity—which rightfully defined simply means *sufficient resources to fulfil your calling plus enough left over to be generous towards others*—doesn't achieve that, then it's a counterfeit, not the real deal.

We of course need to put on the Armour of God to defend ourselves from the flaming arrows of Resheph.[139] But as I've pointed out many times elsewhere, the Armour of God is put on by receiving His kiss. So ask Him for it.

That Armour is mainly defensive, as is the Fruit of the Spirit. Back in the Garden of Eden, fruit was weaponised against humanity; so now, the Fruit of the Spirit is a divine weapon for us against the spirits of the threshold. Just as we can cultivate LOVE to protect us against Python, the spirit of constriction, and JOY to protect us against Ziz, the spirit of forgetting, so we can cultivate PEACE, *shalom*, to protect us against Resheph-Leviathan.

So how do we go about maturing *shalom* in our lives? Two main things: honour and integrity. Honour is discussed at length in the previous book in this series. Honour is like fragrant incense before the throne of

God; dishonour a stench. But what about integrity? At its simplest level, it's simply giving our word and then keeping it. Even when keeping it turns out to be to our disadvantage. It means not breaking it or evading it or looking for a loophole or walking it back. It's no surprise that this used to be called *word of honour*. It means acting with honesty, truth and justice.

If the answer seems too easy, it is. In an ideal world, sure we'd never fail to fend off Leviathan-Resheph with a kiss from God, a song of praise and the wafting fragrance of *shalom*. But this is a fallen world and most of us have a covenant with Death coming down our family lines that offers Resheph unprecedented legal rights to our lives. But hold on—didn't Jesus break the covenant with Death? Wasn't that what the raising of Lazarus was all about? Wasn't that what His own resurrection meant?

In our world where we expect instant fulfilment and gratification, it's easy to overlook that God works in seasons. And that the time indicators in Scripture are there for a reason. Jesus, as we've seen, spent two months in Gilead at Bethany-beyond-the-Jordan, a wadi that in ancient times was called the Brook Cherith—meaning *the cut* and alluding to *the cut of covenant*. John the Baptist used this place not just for its associations with Elijah but because a baptism of repentance here pointed to reaffirmation of covenant.

So when Jesus sought refuge here, He was showing us we must repent and return to covenantal oneness with God. Taking into account the time He took to get there from Jerusalem and then go back to the house of Lazarus, it seems likely He was away for 70 days. That's basically how long it took Him to prepare to break the covenant of Death over the nation. When we want to annul our own covenant with Death, we usually want it done yesterday—or maybe, if we're feeling particularly patient, sometime tomorrow. We look at that 70-day time period and think, 'No way! Can't You shorten the time, Lord?'

Of course, He can—but He probably won't. Because you see, relationships aren't built in a day. Or restored overnight. Commitment takes t-i-m-e.

We begin renewing and restoring our commitment to Jesus by turning aside from our false refuges and seeking Him as our true refuge when the spirit of trouble is pursuing us. The biggest single issue stopping believers from coming into their calling is an unidentified false refuge or two. When we're in strife, we run to some consolation other than the Chief Cornerstone. That false refuge, so Isaiah tells us, is where we'll find evidence of our covenant with Death. He speaks of God's intent to annul this agreement taken out by the people who, terrified of an approaching invasion, took out a spiritual insurance policy:

> *We have made a covenant with Death and a pact with the underworld, so when the overwhelming scourge sweeps over us, it will not harm us. For we have made lies our refuge and find our shelter in falsehood.*
>
> Isaiah 28:15 TPT

Ask God to help you identify and repent of your false refuges. If you're not sure what they are, check out the fourth book in this series, *Hidden in the Cleft: True and*

False Refuge. Until such time as your known false refuges are dismantled and you are tested on your commitment to God, then the covenants in them cannot be annulled. These include, but are not limited to, covenants with Death and the underworld.

In the meantime, follow the example of Jesus: go *into* the 'cut'. He went to a geographic place; but He asks you to go, by faith, into a spiritual place. Ask Him to hide you in the 'cut' in His side, the place where the new birth takes place. It's a place of safety, under His heart, where you can learn to listen to its beat and tune yourself into the cadence of grace. It's a place of honour, of ardent love, of warm comfort. It's a cradle of peace, away from the taunts and mind-crushing twisting of Leviathan and the feverish conflict of Resheph.

In Isaiah 27:1–2, God speaks of the day that He will punish Leviathan and tells us, on that day, to sing of a fruitful vineyard. He says He will be the keeper and watchman of this garden. Like the Garden of Eden which I like to think was sung into being, this garden we are to sing over is our new inheritance. Adam was the steward and keeper of the first garden, but the Lord Himself now guards our inheritance.

But first we have to hand over to Him the rights to do so. We have to ask for the annulment of every covenant with another spirit. We have to put aside wishing in all its forms, including decrees, declarations and 'trading' that are actually attempts to manifest our own desires, not to advance God's calling on our lives. We have to ask Him to identify the counterfeits for us so we can renounce them. We have to draw down contentment from heaven to replace the unquenchable desire to keep on consuming.

We have seen the power of Jesus in His no-holds-barred war-to-the-death against the principalities and threshold guardians. We have seen the conquering of Death itself. And we have also seen the love of Jesus in the way He honoured those we tend to cast in the role of a villain, like Saul, as well as those who were overlooked, like Jephthah's daughter.

Jesus has already done everything necessary to overcome the spirit of trouble in your life. All He's waiting for is your signal to go ahead and apply the power of His cross to your situation. What are you waiting for?

Because, you see, Jesus the cloud-rider is coming back. And He wants His Bride to be ready for Him.

Prayer

It is vitally important to recognise that prayer is about relationship with the Father. None of the prayers in this book are intended as a formula but as a guideline to help you realign yourself with the holy Trinity. They are meant as a starting point for a conversation.

Transformation is only possible as you hold onto the hem of Jesus' prayer shawl and ask Him to mediate before the Father for you. In the end, it's all about Him!

Abba, I want to see my land blessed and healed, and I know You want it too. Yet only Jesus can do the healing. Sometimes, in my enthusiasm or my pity, I petition You for things that are unwise. If I knew more about the history of the situation, I'd ask differently. I forget to ask You what to pray and when.

Remind me always to hold onto the fringe of Jesus' prayer shawl, so He can moderate my presumption and my ignorance.

I know there is truly nothing other than the power of the blood of Jesus when it comes to healing hearts, homes and history. Jesus reversed the transgression of Eden. He conquered the high-ranking spirits who defied You and despoiled them of the royal titles they had claimed. He mended the deep, centuries-long rifts in relationships between nations and peoples.

Jesus can transform my rebellion into love and my insolence into loyalty. I say *yes* and *yes* and *yes* again to His work in me. I know You want me to partner with You in the healing of history but I also know I need to wait for Your signal to 'go'. Help me to align with Your time, Your path, Your strategy and especially Your 'no'. Help me pass the tests.

Lord, I repent of the times I have not trusted You to provide and so have worshipped money and security. I repent of failing to keep Your day holy and so have worshipped time. I repent of dishonouring authority and so have worshipped my own autonomy. I repent of comparing myself with others and so being proud or jealous. I repent of my complicity and my family's complicity with any spirits that defy Your rule and order.

Say the word, Jesus, and I will be healed. Say the word, Jesus, and I will know how to bring healing to my land.

I humbly ask this incomparable blessing in Your name and through the power of Your blood. Amen.

Appendix 1

Summary

RESHEPH IS MENTIONED SEVEN TIMES in Scripture. (SEE ENDNOTE 5) Academically, there is no question that Resheph and Leviathan are different entities. There are no points of connection in any mythology or iconography, nor is there a Scriptural passage that specifically links the two. However on a spiritual plane, it's a different matter. (SEE APPENDIX 2) They are both throne guardians and they occupy the same sacred space; their legal rights to retaliate both derive from dishonour; both of them are overcome by the fruit of *shalom*.

The symbols of Resheph are a gazelle or a stag, arrows, archer, sparks, sirocco, burning coals, thunder/lightning, pestilence, plague, healing, the underworld. It is imaged with a crown decorated with antlers in Egypt, where it is also associated with horses and war. Its titles include 'Lord of the Garden', 'Doorwarden of the Sun' and 'Doorkeeper of the Underworld'.

Jesus confronted Resheph on at least seven occasions.

[1] The raising of Lazarus with its overtones of healing the land from the defilement of Saul's covenant with Sheol.

[2] The resurrection itself with its many evocations of Resheph's iconography including a garden, the fulfilment of the prophecy from the Song of Songs which mentions Resheph and 'migdol' or Magdalene by name as well as a stag, *strong leader*, and the mountain of spices.

[3] Since Resheph is in some places equated with Baal Hadad, the 'cloud-rider', the trial before the Sanhedrin is a crucial challenge. The guilt of Jesus was entirely established on His own testimony to Himself as the 'cloud-rider'. At this point Jesus contests Resheph's claims prior to the resurrection when the complete despoiling occurs of the rituals and liturgies of both Resheph and Hadad.

[4] The emptying of the Temple when the money-changers were driven out. This is a prophecy of the emptying of the

tomb since the only officially sanctioned silver ('keseph' from 'kasaph', *desire*) shekels that could be used to pay the Temple tax had an image of Hercules Melqart, godling of fire and the underworld, on them. It is also a prophetic fulfilment of Isaiah 14:29 which says the Messiah will be like a seraph. (See ENDNOTE 95)

[5] At Caesarea Philippi, in front of the shrine to Pan, Jesus said that the 'Gates of Hades' would not prevail against His church. The common Jewish understanding for 'gates' was *judges* or *rulers*—since, in ancient times, judges and rulers sat at the gates—so Jesus was declaring that the rulers of the underworld, which included Resheph, would not succeed in overcoming the government He instituted in His church.

[6] When Jesus sent out the seventy disciples, He said on their return that He saw the satan fall like lightning from heaven. (Luke 10:17) The image of lightning suggests He was talking about Resheph, a possibility reinforced by His mention of Hades immediately prior to this (Luke 10:15). There is, in my view, a strong case to be made for thinking He made this comment when He was at or near Scythopolis, the foremost town of the Decapolis and the site of the ancient Philistine outpost of Beth Shan.

[7] The naming of James and John as 'sons of thunder' which probably refers to them wanting to call down fire from heaven on a Samaritan village—possibly during the very same ministry where the seventy were sent out on their mission of healing and preaching.

Other possible occasions are:

[1] The time Jesus told Peter to go fishing to get money to pay the Temple tax. The silver coin that was found in the mouth of the fish would have had to have had an image of Hercules Melqart on it. No doubt for a fisherman who was the son of Jonah, it would have symbolised the prophet who was his father's namesake and who'd been delivered up from death and the underworld by a prayer.

[2] His visit to Sychar near Shechem, the place where Resheph was known to be worshipped and where Rehoboam had unwisely commented that he'd whip his forced labour with scorpions.

[3] His visit to Tyre and Sidon, following in the footsteps of Elijah who, like Him, ministered to a Canaanite woman. Elijah of course was the prophet who called down fire from heaven.

Leviathan-Resheph wants to turn our prayers into wishes. Our honour of God through the incense of prayer and praise is changed to a stench of never-sated desire.

Scriptural instances involving Resheph where retaliation for dishonour is apparent are:

- the rebellion of Korah, Dathan and Abiram which involved usurpation of a priestly role.
- the usurpation by Uzziah of the role of the priests.
- the usurpation by Jeroboam of the role the priests.

All of these occurred during offerings of prayer and incense.

Other instances may be:

- the usurpation by Saul of the role of Samuel as a priest
- when Zechariah is struck dumb for doubting the message of the angel Gabriel

Perhaps the most significant instance, however, is the death of Saul and his sons on the day after he covenants with the underworld through necromancy. This is again related to dishonour involving prayer because Saul only took the desperate step of consulting with a medium because he couldn't get an answer from God, no matter what avenue he tried. He found a medium who could call up the dead and asked for Samuel to be brought up from Sheol.

This instance is compounded by David's failure to honour his covenant with the family of Saul; as well as his failure to honour the previous royal family in death. Instead of mending the covenant breach caused by Saul's attack on the Gibeonites, he intensified the problem by adding another covenant breach to the mess. Only when Saul's concubine Rizpah, who has a name with the same meaning as Resheph, *burning coals*, awakens his conscience does the killing famine end.

Jesus takes a hand in mending the actions of both Saul and David during the time when He travels from Bethany-beyond-the-Jordan to Bethany near Jerusalem in order to raise Lazarus from the dead.

Appendix 2

Comparison of Resheph and Leviathan

[1] Resheph is a throne guardian. Leviathan belongs to the Inner Court and is therefore also a throne guardian.

[2] Resheph is a monster of the underworld. Leviathan is a monster of the deep.

[3] Resheph is a seraph. Leviathan is a nachash, and a seraph is also a nachash. This doesn't prove Leviathan is a seraph but strongly suggests the possibility.

[4] Resheph is 'lord of the garden'. Leviathan is a nachash, and a nachash was in the Garden of Eden.

[5] Leviathan is connected to a vineyard; Resheph to a cultivated garden.

[6] Resheph has been linked to Set, the Egyptian godling of the underworld, who is imaged as a jackal. Leviathan has the element 'tan' in its name, meaning *jackal*.

[7] Leviathan is mentioned in Job, implied as the cause of Job's troubles, including disease. In Job, one of the friends connects Resheph with trouble.

[8] Leviathan attends to retaliation for dishonour, Resheph inflicts disease for dishonour. Disease can be a form of retaliation. Both operate primarily within the sacred precinct of the Inner Court.

[9] Leviathan is a flamethrower, from *burning coals*. Resheph is a spark-spitter, from *burning coals*.

[10] Leviathan's name includes 'levi', *joined*, for the *joined scales* of a monster of the deep. Resheph is cognate with Rizpah, which means *joined tiles* as well as *burning coals*.

[11] Leviathan with its many heads is sometimes considered to mean *the wreathed one* or *crowned one*; the antlers of Resheph may perhaps be considered a many-branched crown.

[12] Leviathan is sometimes symbolised by a scorpion or other creature with a stinging tail. Such sharp jabs of poison might be considered the same as the stab of a flaming arrow, since arrows are connected in Resheph's iconography with the toxins of fever.

[13] Leviathan as the 'scorpion' is symbolised by the constellation of Scorpius; the star in the tails are Shaula, *stinger*, and Lesath, *foggy*—note, however, Shaula as a Hebrew word is related to Sheol, *the underworld*, considered to be a land of fog; Resheph as the 'deer' is also symbolised by a constellation, Hercules, which was anciently known as the Stag. Both Scorpius and Hercules are summer constellations in the Northern Hemisphere.

[14] Both Resheph and Leviathan, as throne guardians, are connected to the altar of incense and thus to prayer.

[15] Leviathan is king of the sons of pride, which seems to suggest the 'young lions' who rule over the nations. Baal Hadad, who may be identical with Resheph, is chief of these 'young lions' in Canaanite mythology.

[16] Both Leviathan and Resheph are connected with lines or pathways in the landscape.

[17] Resheph is overcome by the fruit of shalom—prosperity and health. Leviathan is overcome by the fruit of shalom—recompense.

Appendix 3

Some Persian Words

IN PERSIA—WHERE EAST MEETS WEST—we find an extraordinary dictionary list covering many nuances connecting Rizpah, Resheph and Leviathan. In the Book of Esther, the same word used for the *glowing coal* on the altar of incense in Isaiah 6:6 is found in reference to a *mosaic pavement* of alabaster, turquoise, and black-and-white marble. (Esther 1:6) The black marble used in this tiling is 'sochereth', deriving from 'sachar' meaning *travel about, have commercial dealings* or *engage in trade*. It suggests a trading floor and connects the monetary aspects of Resheph's nature first to a tiled pavement, and thence to coals and fire. The black-and-white marble suggests a checkerboard similar to the flooring of a Masonic Lodge which is said to relate back to the design in Solomon's Temple.

Rasaf (Persian) means *joining together stones in a pavement, joining together feet in prayer, agreeing, being suitable.*

> Rizpah (Hebrew) means *joining together stones in a pavement, burning coals, ceremonial stone for incense at the prayer altar.*

> Rasafa, also rsapha (Syriac) and rusafa (Arabic) mean *pavement* with a possible further sense of both *pier* and *embankment* and a poetic sense of *longing for the other bank of the river* (See: Elizabeth Key Fowden, *The Barbarian Plain: Saint Sergius Between Rome and Iran*, University of California Press 1999). All these—*pier*, *embankment* and *other side*—are threshold-related.

Rashf (Persian) means *sipping, sucking, sip, drip*.

Rashaf (Persian) means *sipping*.

> These two words are intriguing for their possible relationship to both 'kaph' and 'saph'—Hebrew for shallow bowl-shaped depressions on a threshold to catch blood dripping from the lintels and doorposts. These words eventually came to

denote the threshold itself and are thought to be the basis of our English words *cup* and *sip* respectively.

Rashk (Persian) means *hitting with an arrow, scribbling of a pen, envy, jealousy*

Rushk (Persian) means *scorpion, brokenness of spirit from jealousy*

These two words unite the idea of Resheph the archer to the scorpion symbol of Leviathan through a link with jealousy.

Appendix 4

On the Jealousy of God

THE JEALOUSY OF GOD in Scripture is not the same as human jealousy. To bring out that significant point, there's a slightly different word in Hebrew to uniquely describe the jealousy of the Lord.

God is jealous for His own name and for its honour, not in the human sense of desiring what others have, but in the divine sense of desiring to give. God will not give honour for dishonour. The eternal principle is that we reap what we sow. As we humble ourselves and honour God, He honours us and exalts us. Conversely, as we exalt ourselves in pride and dishonour Him, we position ourselves for a fall. That tumble may or may not be orchestrated by Leviathan-Resheph.

In being jealous for the sanctity and holiness of His own name, God is indirectly jealous on our behalf. He wants us to partake of His glory.

He enables us to do this through grace. Grace is used in two senses in Scripture but many people think of it only in one way: as the unmerited favour of God. However, the other sense is the empowerment to obey the Law of Christ.

Moses said: Don't kill. Jesus said: Don't get enraged because that is murder in the heart.

Moses said: Don't commit adultery. Jesus said: Don't lust because that is adultery in the heart.

Moses said: Don't be jealous of what your neighbour has. Jesus said: Do good to those who hate you.

Jesus, the Author and Finisher of our faith, didn't come to tear down the Law: He came to make it a *minimum* requirement. He came to make it incomparably higher. He came to give us the grace of His Father and the empowerment of His cross to honour God through an obedience just like His.

Endnotes

1. See *Like Wildflowers, Suddenly* for details on Asherah and Tammuz, as well as Dagon, the grain-and-fish deity of the Philistines and also the deified hero, Julius Caesar. Jesus confronted Dagon and Tammuz simultaneously; then later took on Dionysius, the so-called True Vine (see Peter Jones, *On Global Wizardry: Techniques of Pagan Spirituality and a Christian Response*, Main Entry Editions 2010, p 82) at the same time as He did Julius Caesar. These are just a few of His many battles against those human beings and spiritual entities who claimed powers and privileges belonging only to His Father.

2. Looking back, I can see how often the Spirit of God protected me. I was a voracious reader. It was my general rule always to finish any book I started. But something always stopped me reading Alan Garner's *Elidor*. The title was attractive, the cover illustration alluring, the opening scene enticing—and I think I got to page 3 on four or five different occasions before closing the book and deciding not to go further. Finally, as an adult, I began to wonder what was in it that caused those inexplicable halts. When at last God gave me permission to read the book, I realised He'd messaged me repeatedly whenever I'd succumbed to picking it up again in order to keep me safe. The theme of the story, as a child or even a teenager, would have destroyed me. It was simply: *the witch can never be defeated—she will always return.*

3. George MacDonald, *At the Back of the North Wind*, London, 1871

4. Literary commentators often see the North Wind as a symbol of Death. I can see how they come to this conclusion but I think it's ultimately the result of our culturally refined 'nice' view of God. It's just like expecting Aslan to be a tame lion. It doesn't take account of MacDonald's views of God as having both mother and father attributes—views so important to him that he lost his church benefice over it; nor does it take account of the varying qualities of a mother: it seems to expect her to be always warm and nurturing but never fierce.

5. Deuteronomy 32:24 *pestilence*; Job 5:7 *flying sparks*; Psalm 76:3 *burning arrows*; Psalm 78:48 *sirocco*; Song of Songs 8:6 (twice) *burning coals*; Habakkuk 3:5 *sirocco*

6. Patrick M. Arnold, *Gibeah: The Search for a Biblical City*, Sheffield Academic Press, 1990

7. The deceit started with Abram when he was in Egypt and persuaded Sarai to say she was his sister. Although God gave Abraham a second chance at this test when he and Sarah went to Gerar, he still failed to trust God and again asked his wife to say she was his sister. Isaac was given a chance to pass the test his father had failed but he too was deceitful. Consequently, deceit became the unresolved generational iniquity and Jacob was named for it, making it the front-and-centre problem. Every time Isaac and Rebekah used his name they should have been reminded of their own failings. Yet, like other parents who name their sons and daughters for unresolved issues, they are also prophesying to the children that they are the ones to bring the problem to an end. In the next generation, Jacob accepted the name Joseph, chosen by his wife Rachel, for his son. She clearly intended it as a prophecy of more children, since Joseph means *he adds*. However all names have inbuilt choices, and these always have both negative and positive overtones. In context therefore, Joseph ben Jacob could be seen as *Manipulator, son of Deceiver*. Fortunately Joseph learns integrity the hard way and the positive overtones of his name come to the fore. *He adds* also has a sense of *building a treasury* and that's exactly what Joseph does in Egypt: he builds storehouses of grain in provision against the coming seven-year famine.

8. Saul means *desire* or *prayed for*, but both it and Sheol, *hell*, derive from 'shaal', *to ask*. Add a K in the front of Sheol and the result is the Hebrew phrase, 'as Sheol'—but that K prefixed to the SH produces KSH, which sounds just like Kish, the name of Saul's father. The previous word, *unrelenting*, or in some versions *cruel*, actually sounds even closer to this name because it starts with a Q, just as the original Hebrew does. In fact, however, if we're being truly pedantic, Kish in Hebrew doesn't start with a K. That's just the English transliteration. In Hebrew, Kish starts with a Q. But not to worry, because the previous word, *unrelenting*, starts with 'qsh' anyway. *Unrelenting* (qshh) seems to be a deliberate reminder of Kish(q'sh).

9. The name, Qos, is found in the Nabataean language in an inscription at Khirbet et-Tannur, where he is represented flanked by bulls, seated on a throne while wielding in his left hand a multi-pronged thunderbolt, suggestive of a function as a weather god (en.wikipedia.org/wiki/Qos_(deity) — accessed 22 May 2020)

10. Joseph Blenkinsopp, *Gibeon and Israel: The Role of Gibeon and the Gibeonites in the Political and Religious History of Early Israel*, The Society for Old Testament Study, Monograph Series 1972

11. arabianprophets.com/?page_id=2081 (accessed 6 July 2020)

12. Lata Bothra in *Jainism: An Image of Antiquity* considered that Rishabha the teacher and 'ford-maker' of the Jain religion was, in the west, worshipped as Resheph. See: latabothra.in/images/An_Antiquty_of_Jainism.pdf (accessed 10 March 2020)

13. I love reading fantasy. And I love writing fantasy. And the main reason I love it is because it enables the expression of ideas that are in the Scriptures but are hidden by the relentless push for easy-to-read culturally relevant translations. For example, in Ray Hawkins' devotional, *The Warrior Lord's Sword*, he pointed out that, in Hebrews 4:12, 'double-edged' is actually 'double-mouthed'. It's about blessing and cursing from the same source. I instantly thought of the double-function swords and spears of mythology and fantasy—the ones that both wound and heal. It's easy to miss how many unusual ideas of great fantasy have their source in the Scriptures. The idea of wounding and healing coming from the same source is very significant for any study of Resheph who is seen as both bringing disease as well as healing.

14. Besides bringing pestilence, Resheph also allegedly had the power to heal disease. The Phoenicians considered him to be *lord of the arrow* as well as *lord of the garden*. In Egypt, he was associated with antelopes and horses and was represented in hieroglyphics with a crown ornamented with a gazelle skull. In Hittite and Syrian culture, he was associated with the stag. In my view, this strange conglomeration of a thunder god wearing antlers might suggest this headgear is a symbol of forked lightning.

15. *'To whom is all the desire of Israel turned, if not to you and your whole family line?'* 1 Samuel 9:20 NIV

16. In describing the reigns of the kings of Edom, it was recorded: *'Samlah died, and Shaul of Rehoboth on the Euphrates reigned in his place.'* Genesis 36:37 ESV

17. The story of Michal, the daughter of Saul and wife of David, is a complex one. Like her brother Jonathan, she defends David at the risk of her own life. Saul used David's desire to marry her to try to get him killed—he made the brideprice a hundred Philistine foreskins. Despite her betrothal to David, she was given to another man in marriage and she apparently bore him five sons—though it is sometimes said she fostered these sons and they were actually her nephews. Eventually she returned to David, but she had no

children by him (and this is sometimes thought to mean she had no children at all, hence the question over whether the sons of the former marriage were her own or foster children). The critical incident that seems to be a deciding factor in this lack of children is her heart's reaction as she watched David dance before the Ark of the Covenant as it was brought into Jerusalem. Immediately after David explains himself to her, the comment is made: *'And Michal daughter of Saul had no children to the day of her death.'* (2 Samuel 6:23 NIV) This comment seems to suggest that her childlessness was a direct consequence of her attitude. A superficial reading would see this as a punishment from God. But a deeper reading would see this as David's unforgiveness and refusal to have anything more to do with her. Perhaps it even comes from the heart of Michal herself. The name Michal sounds like 'machol', *dancing*. In despising what David was doing, she despised her own identity, her own calling, her own self. She hated the defilement by David of her name, and perhaps further hated her own name. When we hate our own name, we are like Michal—we hate the calling God has placed over our lives and we are unwilling and thus unable to give birth to it. However Michal doesn't just sound like 'machol', *dancing*, but is the same as 'mikal', *brook* (see Endnote 67) and Mekal, the deity of the town of Beth Shan who was elsewhere identified with Resheph. Saul's family, beginning long before his own time, had very ambiguous names. On the one hand, they seemed innocuous (Saul: *prayed for*; *long desired*) but on the other hand devoted to other deities (Saul: *Sheol*; *hell*). The entire family is named for godlings of the underworld, Michal included. No wonder she hated her name.

18. Also spelled Mikel.

19. Also spelled *Beit She'an*, *Bet She'an*, *Beth-Shan*, *Baysan*, or *Beisan*. Beth Shan is used here because it is the spelling used in connection with the death of Saul.

20. An inscription was found at Ialium in Cyprus identifying Resheph as Mekal. See: Henry O. Thompson, *Mekal—The God of Beth Shan*, E.J. Brill, 1970

21. There's a flicker of a connection between the patriarch Benjamin himself and the Edomites, but it does not seem to endure through the following generations. Benjamin's firstborn son was Bela, *swallow suddenly, engulf, eat, devour, destroy*. It is the same name as one of the kings of Edom, and is also the proper name of Zoar, the city of the plain that Lot fled to as Sodom was destroyed.

22. Her sister, Merab, has a name usually translated *increase* or *multiplication* or *agent of greatness* from 'rabab', *abundance*. However, the other possible root is 'rab', *chief* or *archer*. Would it not be likely that Saul named his daughter in honour of his father and so they both have a name with a similar connotation? Yet again indirectly pointing to the archer godling of the underworld, Resheph? Poetically, it is also a close assonance for 'maarab', *the west*, from 'ereb', *evening*, from 'oreb', *raven*. But just to keep us on our toes, 'mereb' and 'ereb' also refer to Arabia and to *a mixture of peoples*. Edom bordered the Arabian Desert and, in the time of Jesus, if not before, Arabia was synonymous with the ancient Edomite kingdom, not with the present nation of Saudi Arabia. It is
23. therefore possible that Merab's name was another link to Edom.

24. Also spelled Jehonathan.

25. If you've suspected a relationship between Micah and Mekal who is otherwise Resheph, you'd be right.

26. The word 'kesheph' in Hebrew has the letter 'shin', while 'keseph' has a 'samekh'. Since this book is about thresholds and the guardians that watch over them, it should be further pointed out that 'kasaph', *desire*, from which 'keseph' originates has one of the words for *threshold*, 'saph', encoded in it.

27. My apologies for the story in *God's Poetry* about Saul under a pomegranate tree. I have since come across Patrick Arnold's book on Gibeah which makes a very compelling case for a cave in the wilderness, just a few kilometres from Gibeah.

28. Patrick M. Arnold, *Gibeah: The Search for a Biblical City*, Sheffield Academic Press, 1990.

29. Assuming Jaba' is Gibeah and Beitin is Bethel.

30. Almond is a threshold symbol because traditionally the almond tree is the first to 'wake up' after winter in Israel and bring forth blossoms. It's a signal on the threshold of spring as the year passes from one season to the next. The connotation of almond, 'shaqad', is *watching, being on the lookout, wakeful, staying awake,* or *remaining alert.*

31. abarim-publications.com/Meaning/Luz.html (accessed 23 May 2020)

The other issue that might hang over Jerusalem in terms of defilement arises from the fact that David may have dishonoured the people of Benjamin by setting up his capital at Jerusalem. The city of Jebus which he took was in the territory of Benjamin. Should he have handed it over to them? After all, he belonged to the tribe of Judah. Was conquest enough to give him the rights of possession? I'm not sure but I think it highly possible that, in the long feud between the people of Bethlehem and the people of Gibeah, this was simply another episode of one-upmanship.

32. abarim-publications.com/Bible_Commentary/Hair_words.html (accessed 21 May 2020)

33. The word used is 'saphah', *to be swept away* or *caught up*, from 'saph', *threshold*.

34. Michael S. Heiser, *The Unseen Realm: Recovering the Supernatural Worldview of the Bible*, Lexham Press 2015, quoting *Dictionary of Demons in the Bible*.

35. Although Korah was a Levite, his allies were not.

36. It may well be that Aaron's sons, Nadab and Abihu, who died for offering strange fire received retaliation for dishonouring God by failing to follow His ordinances in the place of prayer.

37. The word for *withered* here is 'bosh', *to dry up* or *be ashamed*. The same element occurs in Ja*besh*.

38. Brian Simmons, *The Passion Translation, Isaiah: The Vision*, Broadstreet Publishing Group 2018. Simmons spells 'rizpah' as 'ritzpah'.

39. The word 'resheph' is in fact derived from 'saraph', *burn* or *live coal*, which has the same Hebrew spelling as its intimate relation, 'seraph', *six-winged angelic being*. Besides *live coal*, 'resheph' can also be translated as *lightning*, *fire-bolt*, *flashing arrow*, *spark*, *burning fever* or *plague*. Another Hebrew word also meaning *live coal* is 'rizpah'.

40. Although the medieval hierarchy of angels is still often—but by no means universally—followed today, the distinctions in the Bible are not always clear. Are the cherubim and seraphim different classes of angels or is one a sub-group of the other? Or does the description simply indicate their function? Contemporary references are not particularly helpful: the winged griffins of Egypt called 'seraf', for example, which transported prayers to 'heaven' (as well as deceased Pharaohs) were sometimes considered cherubim. jewishencyclopedia.com/articles/13437-seraphim and also

bibleodyssey.org/en/tools/ask-a-scholar/seraphs (accessed 11 August 2020)

41. Michael S. Heiser, *Demons: What the Bible Really Says About The Powers of Darkness*, Lexham Press 2020

42. Strictly speaking, my current count of 70 (which is ongoing) includes deified culture heroes such as Moses or Julius Caesar. I include these, as well as the members of various pantheons, because in the case of Julius Caesar, he was considered a god after his death. I further include Moses because Jesus made the extraordinary statement that it was not Moses who gave manna to the people in the wilderness, but God. If He actually had to make a comment of that nature, then it follows that some of His listeners viewed Moses as more than human.

43. In addition, it could perhaps be considered that Rachel was weeping too over the descendants of her son, Joseph. He had two sons, Manasseh and Ephraim. The younger son Ephraim was the ancestor of Jeroboam who led the revolt against Solomon's son, Rehoboam, and split the Kingdom of David into two sections: the Kingdom of Judah and the Kingdom of Israel. This northern kingdom was sometimes simply called 'Ephraim' and, from the start, was apostate: in rebellion against God. These two kingdoms were never reunified until the day Jesus sat by a well in Samaria.

44. Let's not forget Saul the Pharisee either who raged against the followers of Jesus, in a similar way to his namesake's rage against Jesus' forebear, David.

45. See both behindthename.com/name/herod and also abarim-publications.com/Meaning/Herod.html (accessed 8 June 2020)

46. In both 2007 and 2011, fights between rival groups of priests with brooms broke out, resulting in injuries to bystanders. The church is jointly administered by Roman Catholic, Greek Orthodox and Armenian Apostolic authorities. CBS News reported: 'Any perceived encroachment on one group's turf can set off vicious feuds.' cbsnews.com/news/priests-brawl-at-holy-church-in-bethlehem/ (accessed 13 June 2020)

47. abarim-publications.com/Meaning/Helkath-hazzurim.html (accessed 10 January 2020)

48. The spirit of Lilith is allied not only with Belial but also with the underworld. The name Lilith comes from 'layil', *night*, from 'luwl', *a twisting* (away of the light), *midnight season*, metaphorically *adversity*.

49. Samuel's father came from the hill country of Ephraim, as indicated in the very first verse of the first book of Samuel. The significance of Saul's friendship with Samuel should not be pushed to the background: it was sufficient reason for deep suspicion by the people of Bethlehem who saw the alliance between the king and the seer as a source of potential trouble. When Samuel turned up one day looking to anoint one of Jesse's sons, they clearly wondered if he'd come in peace; or whether some pretext for another episode in the ongoing war between Bethlehem and Gibeah was about to be revealed.

50. See *Dealing with Python: Spirit of Constriction, Strategies for the Threshold #1*, Armour Books 2017.

51. It was routine for a chieftain and his armour-bearer to have cut a blood covenant together. This explains why the Philistine king Achish who appointed David as his bodyguard was willing to invest so much trust in him.

52. 2 Samuel 9:1 ESV

53. '*The body must not remain hanging from the tree overnight. You must bury the body that same day, for anyone who is hung is cursed in the sight of God. In this way, you will prevent the defilement of the land the Lord your God is giving you as your special possession.*' (Deuteronomy 20:23 NLT) Although this verse specifically refers to defiling the land because of a curse on a *hanged* body, the general principle for the Israelites was (and is) to bury the body the same day to avoid defilement.

54. It's interesting to realise that Nathan's story about the lamb quickened David's conscience, while Joab's subtle criticism of David (in 2 Samuel 11:21) through another story failed to do so. In this story about the death of Gideon's son Abimelech, Joab renamed Gideon 'Jerubbesheth', *let shame contend with him*. Joab thereby implied that David, who was his uncle, should be ashamed of his behaviour. Not only that, he was also drawing a comparison between David and his former rival Ish-bosheth, *man of shame*. Ish-bosheth was the son of Saul who had briefly reigned after his father's death and who had only lost hold of power when Abner no longer supported him. By using this name for Gideon, Joab was

saying to David: 'Let shame contend with you. You have become unworthy to rule. This is not the behaviour our family expects of an honourable man.'

55. Genesis 36:24

56. It seems that, as a Hebrew word, Resheph is conceived of as coming from 'rosh', *head* or *chief*, together with 'apher', *covering*, from "epher', *ashes*. However, the other likely nuances here are 'sheph', *swept bare* or *judgment* which not only rhymes with 'saph', *threshold*, but is cognate with 'saphah', *swept away* (which actually derives from 'saph'). In addition, it also rhymes with 'kaph', *cornerstone* or *threshold*. If there is a resonance in the name Resheph that points to *chief cornerstone*, then the name must not only go back to the original hearth of the family altar (see Henry Clay Trumbull, *The Threshold Covenant or The Beginning of Religious Rites*) but it is also evident that Resheph is a counterfeit of Jesus as the Chief Cornerstone.

57. Kish in Hebrew starts with a Q and Cush with a K. Nevertheless the similarity of sound suggests this identification.

58. The translation of the Hebrew Scriptures into Greek in the second or third century before Christ.

59. abarim-publications.com/Meaning/Cush.html (accessed 1 August 2020)

60. Rabbi Yechiel Eckstein said: 'The Sages offer two possibilities. The first is when David sang a song of praise to God after Saul was finally killed at the hands of the Philistines.' It was inappropriate to celebrate the death of an anointed king—lament was appropriate. The second possibility, according to Eckstein, is when David cut off a piece of Saul's robe. Saul didn't know David was hiding in the cave and David could have killed him, as his men were urging. Instead David spared Saul's life but took a piece of his cloak in order to prove his good intentions. Eckstein points out: 'Again... his actions were still wrong because he had lifted a hand against God's appointed king of Israel.' My view is to the contrary. David's comment to his men indicates, to me, he was *refusing* to lift his hand against the Lord's anointed.

61. If Tishbe, *settlers*, is indeed in the Brook Cherith, then Elijah would have been very familiar with the caves and crannies of the valley, so it was a natural choice for a hide-out.

62. Kenneth K. A. Silver in *He Walked On 'The Other Side' Of The River Jordan: The Early Church In Ancient Israel And Beyond The River Jordan In The 1st To The 4th Century AD* in *ARAM* 29: 1&2 (2017) quotes Samuel Tobias Lachs, *A Rabbinic Commentary on the New Testament, The Gospels of Matthew, Mark, and Luke* (New York, New Jersey: Ktav Publishing House, Inc., Hoboken New Jersey, Anti-Defamation League of B'nai B'rith, 1987) who says: '"beyond the Jordan" also had a specific meaning the importance of which has largely been neglected: it is synonymous with Perea, i.e. the area between the rivers Arnon and the Jabbok.' In the time of Herod the Great, the area of Perea, *the land beyond*, was a territory on the eastern bank of the Jordan stretching from just south of Pella to the middle of the eastern shore of the Dead Sea. The brook Cherith, lying just south of Pella, would therefore have been near to the northern boundary of Perea. It may even have formed the boundary.

63. Furthermore it qualifies as the famous 'Refuge in Edom' predicted by Daniel in his end-times vision. Daniel prophesied that, when the King of the North invades the 'Beautiful Land': *'These shall be delivered out of his hand: Edom and Moab and the main part of the Ammonites.'* (Daniel 11:41 ESV) In fact, while this verse speaks of what is classed by scholars as the 'Refuge in Edom', it's clear the place of deliverance is not restricted to Edom. It could also be Moab or Ammon. The Brook Cherith certainly meets that criteria because it was indeed in the ancient territory of the Ammonites.

64. It is also linked to the name of the metal serpent Nehushtan (or Nechushtan).

65. jewishencyclopedia.com/articles/11276-nahash (accessed 6 June 2020)

66. It's difficult to tell the significance of tamarisk trees in Scripture. The first time one is mentioned is when Abraham plants one after covenanting with Abimelech and Phicol. Based on its uses in Mesopotamia (Abraham's origin), it seems to have been for purification and exorcism. This would make sense in Jabesh Gilead where the men would have wanted both to purify the bodies of Saul and his sons from the defilement they'd suffered in the Philistine temple, and also to exorcise any spirits that may have attached themselves through any pagan dedication. They may also have been concerned about witchcraft, if they had heard about Saul's action in visiting the witch of Endor the day before his final battle. If purification and exorcism were their motives, this indicates how thoughtful they were in honouring the bodies, even in death.

67. Her name is spelled the same way as 'mikal', *brook* or *streamlet*, and it rhymes with 'maqqal', *rod*, *branch* or *staff*. There are forty natural water springs near Beit She'an and many small streams. The suggestive phrasing of Scripture hints that Michal, as David's wife, is childless in retaliation for contempt. It does not say she was barren, suggesting it was David's decision not to approach her. His intent might have been to honour God, but his lewd actions and unrepentant attitude undermined that desire. Nonetheless Michal was wrong to despise him. She should have known better than to dishonour anyone. After all, she was a Benjaminite, and thus descended from the women of Jabesh Gilead.

68. In Cyprus, Resheph and Mekal are identified as the same deity.

69. Jabesh-Gilead (said to mean *dry place of Gilead*) was a prominent Israelite city during the period of Judges and the monarchy. According to the Jewish Virtual Library, 'its inhabitants appear to have had close ties with the tribe of Benjamin because they did not join the expedition of the Israelite tribes against Benjamin and because, when the city was besieged by Nahash king of Ammon, it appealed for help to Saul the Benjamite who assembled the army of Israel at Bezek, reached Jabesh-Gilead after a day's march, and routed the Ammonites (1 Samuel 11). Out of gratitude the men of Jabesh-Gilead went to Beth-Shan where the bodies of Saul and his sons had been hung on its wall after their defeat at Mount Gilboa, removed the bodies, and buried them under a tamarisk in their territory (1 Samuel 31:11–13; 1 Chronicles 10:11–12). For this deed of valour and mercy they were highly praised by David (2 Samuel 2:4–6). Some scholars suggest Elijah should be "the Jabeshite" (*ha-Yaveshi*) instead of "the Tishbite" (*ha-Tishbi*). The name Jabesh-Gilead has been preserved in the name of Wadi Yābis, a tributary of the Jordan 6 km south of Pella. Eusebius locates it six Roman miles south of Pella on the road to Gerasa (*Onomasticon* 110:11ff.) Its accepted identification is with Tell al-Maqlūb; Glueck has proposed Tell Abu Kharaz as the site of Israelite Jabesh-Gilead and Tell al-Maqbara farther down the wadi as the Roman-Byzantine city; these identifications, however, disregard Eusebius' statement. Tell el-Maqlub might be a better candidate for Elisha's home town of Abel-me-holah (1 Kings 19:16). The double mounds of Tell el-Meqbereh and Tell Abu Kharaz have produced surface pottery of the period of Saul and stand near enough to the Jordan—in fact, on the edge of the valley itself—to fit well the story of the recovery of Saul and Jonathan's bodies.' (jewishvirtuallibrary.org/jabesh-gilead — accessed 11 August 2019)

70. See abarim-publications.com/Meaning/Jabesh.html for this interpretation of 'besh' as *humility*, rather than *shame*. Certainly it makes more sense for Saul's sons to have been named for *humility*, rather than *shame*. (Yes, even despite having the entire progenitor of the Israelites being called Jacob, *deceiver*.) It's actually worth considering that the people of Jabesh Gilead were always honourable, even those who were wiped out because they didn't turn up to the war against Benjamin. Perhaps they were the only honourable ones in all Israel! The action of Jonathan the Levite in sending around pieces of a human body as a call to war was totally perverse. The elders of Jabesh Gilead may have (rightly) concluded it was exactly that—obscene and illegitimate—and that the defilement it represented meant any war was not going to go well. If they did abstain from involving themselves in the internecine warfare for honourable motives, it didn't save them in the end. Just because we're honourable doesn't mean it will always go well with us. Jesus, after all, promised us 'besh', *persecution*.

71. Wish activation is not confined to these elements. It also includes cracking a wishbone, making a wishlist, creating a wishing tree and such symbols as a magic lamp.

72. Jesus warns specifically against this in Matthew 6:7 NLT: *'When you pray, don't babble on and on as the Gentiles do. They think their prayers are answered merely by repeating their words again and again.'*

73. *Labyrinth* is thought to mean *house of the double axe*. A priestly class at Delphi was named similarly; suggesting the labyrinth is connected with Python Apollo. In the Middle Ages, labyrinths and mazes were connected with the name Gillian or Julian ('Gillian's Bore' or 'Julian Bower', sometimes 'July Park'), or sometimes called 'Troytown' or 'The Walls of Troy'. Celtic historians associate it with the journey of the dead into the afterlife. The purpose of the labyrinth in modern spirituality is to produce union with the divine (Peter Jones, *One or Two? Seeing a World of Difference*, Main Entry Editions 2010). It therefore seeks to reproduce the end result of covenant with God, without actually assenting to the pledges and promises of covenant..

74. Of course the first faint echoes of this raven-dove symbolism are found in the two birds sent out by Noah. The raven, as a death-eater, does not need to return to the ark for food; but the dove does.

75. See the discussion of the relationship between 'miphtan' and 'pethen', *python*, in *Dealing with Python: Spirit of Constriction, Strategies for the Threshold #1*, Armour Books 2017.

76. Also spelled Seila. During the medieval period, a ritual called 'tekufab' was performed in memory of Jephthah's daughter. It involved *not* drinking from wells during certain hours on four days during the year: the summer and winter solstices as well as the two equinoxes.

77. This occurred at Shechem where Resheph was known to be worshipped. Resheph was also worshipped at Ebla in Syria and at Byblos in Lebanon. The young prince Shechem, after whom the city seems to have been named—or perhaps it was the reverse and he was named for the city—was willing to be circumcised in order to marry Dinah. That is, he agreed to come within the covenant. Levi and Simeon, in slaying the citizens of Shechem, totally desecrated that covenant. Shechem, the city, had five major ratifications of covenant with Yahweh over its history—so it is little wonder the locality had a shrine to Baal Berith, *god of the covenant*.

78. Zela, *rib*, *side* (Hebrew), is related to ala, *rib* (Aramaic).

79. It may formerly have been Zilu or Zela Haeleph, *ox-rib*.

80. Bethany on the eastern slope of the Mount of Olives is now identified with the suburb of Al-Eizariya (Al-Azariya), from El'Azir (*Lazarus*).

81. See the third book in this series, *Name Covenant: Invitation to Friendship, Strategies for the Threshold #3*, Armour Books 2018.

82. Some people get hung up on the etymology—a word's meaning as derived from its original language—when analysing a name. God, in my experience, is not nearly so picky. Maybe because He's a poet, as Ephesians 2:10 tells us.

83. Like Saul's family who assumed the names of the godlings of Edom, Esther and her uncle Mordecai took on the names of pagan deities: Ishtar and Marduk from the Babylonian pantheon. These names cannot be excused on the basis of trying to fit in locally, since they were in Persia at the time, not Babylon.

84. Mentioned in Esther 4:16.

85. Even though I suspect this is about Esther, something in my heart can't quite let go of the thought there is also something in His delay going back to the very beginning of the story of Jabesh Gilead—

when none of the men of the town turned up for the war against Gibeah and the tribe of Benjamin. However, I can't articulate the thought that lies behind this suspicion. Alternatively (or rather, since this *is* Jesus after all, *in addition*) perhaps it's in some way related to the seven days of purification undertaken by the men of Jabesh Gilead after retrieving Saul's body from Beth Shan. It seems to be six or seven days between the time Jesus gets the message at Bethany-beyond-the-Jordan and His arrival at Bethany.

86. According to Talmudists, Nergal means *dunghill cock*. But that seems more like propaganda than poetry.

87. There are echoes from Isaiah in Jesus' statement about stumbling in the darkness: '*In the past He humbled the land of Zebulun and the land of Naphtali, but in the future He will honour the Way of the Sea, beyond the Jordan, Galilee of the nations: The people walking in darkness have seen a great light; on those living in the land of the shadow of death, a light has dawned.*' (Isaiah 9:1–2 BSB) The lands of Zebulun and Naphtali were the first to fall to the Assyrian invasion, but those regions as well as Caesarea Philippi on the Way of the Sea, Gilead ('beyond the Jordan') and Galilee saw the first work of Christ as He healed people and history. Jesus used a good rabbinical technique in talking about 'walking in darkness': the disciples were probably supposed to quote the next line and conclude from its reference to the shadow of death what had happened to Lazarus. But it was a bit too allusive.

88. Beit She'an in the time of Jesus was Scythopolis, the largest town of the Decapolis. Not far away were the villages of Aenon and Salim where John the Baptist moved his ministry because of their plentiful water. This is the other side of the river to the Brook Cherith where he began his ministry at Bethany-beyond-the-Jordan. It is also the 'evening' (areb) side of the river to the place where ravens (oreb) came. Today the river at this point is bridged by the Sheik Hussein/Jordan River Crossing.

89. Amos 8:1–2.

90. Michael Heiser, *Old Testament Pagan Divination* in *On Global Wizardry: Techniques of Pagan Spirituality and a Christian Response*, Peter Jones (ed.), Main Entry Editions 2010. He also distinguishes between 'passing through the fire' and actually sacrificing a child as a burnt offering. These subtle distinctions may have informed the understanding of witchcraft in the Middle Ages as a sign of weakness in faith. It is only when witchcraft became linked to

heresy (ironically in the time of the 'Enlightenment') that the great persecutions of witches began. See Jeffrey Burton Russell, *Witchcraft in the Middle Ages*, Cornell University Press 1984

91. My mother was taken to Culloden Moor while visiting Scotland. She had no idea it was a battlefield but, on arriving, was struck with a sense of horror. 'They're not dead!' she cried. The owner of a nearby bookstore said he did a very good trade because of people with sensitivities like hers. Their friends tended to leave them behind to browse the bookstore while traipsing around the battlefield.

92. John 14:6.

93. *The Lion, the Witch and the Wardrobe* in *The Chronicles of Narnia*.

94. Ezekiel 28:16. See *God's Pottery: The Sea of Names and the Pierced Inheritance*, Armour Books 2016, where I have made the suggestion that this verse refers to trading in names: thus in callings, destinies and identities.

95. They may also have fulfilled a prophecy—that of Isaiah 14:29–30. This mind-blowing oracle against the Philistines suggests, in Hebrew if not in English, that the Messiah will be like one of the seraphim. That is, the Messiah would be like a winged serpent of flames and fire! Assuming that such a prophecy is meant functionally and not physically then, to be like this, the Messiah would have to assume an official role like one of these heavenly courtiers. He would therefore have to take charge of ensuring the holiness of God's temple was maintained and would further mean He would have to remove those who trample on the consecration of the courts. To be like one of these seraphic threshold guardians, He would have to expel the unsanctified with flicking and lashing. Jesus did precisely this when He made His whip—which is like the stinging tail of Leviathan. While Leviathan is not mentioned by name in Isaiah 14:29, it could well be referred to, since the word 'nachash' is. The 'nachash' could of course also refer to Nehushtan, the bronze serpent that Moses had made at God's command, but which Hezekiah destroyed because it had become an idol.

96. Some commentators think Jesus cleared out the Temple *twice* because the event is mentioned at the end of Matthew's gospel but at the beginning of John's. However, no time-stamp is on John's account—and in his earlier scenes there are clear chronological markers—so I believe he has deliberately framed this account to counterpoint the empty tomb. The pairing of scenes throughout

John's gospel, front and back, is very Hebrew in conception—it's a poetic device called chiasmus. There are, as pointed out in *God's Pottery: The Sea of Names and the Pierced Inheritance*, Armour Books 2016, at least 22 of these pairs, many of them featuring people with identical names.

97. A one-to-one association has existed between Heracles and Melqart since Herodotus described the 'Pillars of Melqart' at the western end of the Mediterranean Sea. The pillars in the temple near Gades/Gádeira (modern Cádiz) have sometimes been considered to be the true *Pillars of Hercules*, rather than the geographical headlands. en.wikipedia.org/wiki/Pillars_of_Hercules (accessed 20 June 2020)

98. As a pillar, Boaz has the connotation of *belief*. In the famous verse, Genesis 15:6 NIV, '*Abram believed the Lord and He credited to him as righteousness*,' the word usually translated *believed* is the first occasion in Scripture we find 'aman' being used. It has many connotations: *confirm, establish, support, secure, pillar, faithful, foster-father, foster-mother, nurse, nurturer, nourisher*. Because today we often think of 'belief' as intellectual assent rather than faith that is actively invested in advancing God's kingdom, perhaps this verse sometimes gives the wrong impression to modern Christians. Therefore, 'Abram made the Lord the foundational pillar of his life and God credited it to him as righteousness' comes closer to the mark.

99. Similar to Maori beliefs about carved posts on a marae.

100. Boaz and Jachin are usually translated *strength* and *established*, but I've always felt there was more to it than was obvious. After long research I believe the names are allusive references to the morning and evening star. Erik Langkjer in *The Origin of Our Belief in God* connects Boaz to the morning star. His identification makes sense given the notorious difficulty of translating 'ayil', Hebrew for *strong leader*. In *God's Panoply: The Armour of God and the Kiss of Heaven*, Armour Books 2016, I have noted 'ayil' can be translated *ram, oak, post* or *mighty man* and that its feminine form is actually part of the Hebrew name for the morning star. Langkjer suggests Bo'az is a cognate for 'Azizu, *strong one*, an Arabic name for *the morning star*. Likewise Jachin as the evening star relies on a subtle parallel. Before Jachin was used as the name of a temple pillar, it was the name of one of the sons of Simeon. This son was also called Jarib (compare 1 Chronicles 4:24 with Genesis 46:10), said to mean *God contends*.

101. Jarib however rhymes with "ereb', *evening*, from a root meaning *surety*. Thus *evening* has also got a similar subtly allusive feel to Jachin, *he will (securely) establish*.

    John 11:39 KJV. When I was working as an editor of a devotional magazine, part of my job was to ensure the language wasn't too archaic and to remove, if necessary, quotes from the King James Version of the Bible in favour of the New King James Version. But when it came to John 11:39, there was simply no adequate substitute for Martha's protest, 'He stinketh!' So it's the one verse that, despite its old-fashioned language, always stayed!

102. For the Roman soldiers outside the tomb, the myrrh must have been unsettling. Particularly when the angel arrived, sat on the rolled-back stone and an earthquake occurred. Theocritus related the legend of a Greek goddess named Angelos, *angel*, who was the daughter of Zeus and Hera. When she grew up she stole the myrrh that Hera used on her face. Hera pursued her but gave up when she hid with some corpse-bearers. She eventually became connected with the underworld. So the appearance of an angel and the aroma of myrrh at a tomb—a traditional 'entrance to the underworld'—probably terrified them into thinking they were about to be dragged down to Hades.

103. The pierced messiah seems to have been a traditional belief not unlike that of the royal messiah and the war messiah. A six-line fragment, commonly referred to as the 'Pierced Messiah' text, is written in a Herodian script of the first half of the 1st Century and refers to the 'stump of Jesse'—the Messiah—from the Branch of David, to a judgment, killing, and cleansing of the land of the dead by the Messiah's soldiers.

104. Many constellations were associated with the adventures of Heracles, *glory of the air*, who had his labours represented amongst the stars of heaven. The notion was apparently adopted from the star myths of the so-called 'Phoenician Heracles', the hero-god of Lebanon known as Melqart. A number of his labours, missing from the Greek stellar arrangements, are considered recognisable in their older Eastern forms. The adventures of Heracles can be paired with the following constellations: (1) the Nemean Lion, constellation Leo; (2) the Hydra and Crab, constellations Hydra and Cancer; (3) the Stymphalian Birds, constellations Lyra and Cygnus; (4) the Cretan Bull, constellation Taurus; (5) the Hesperian Dragon, constellation Serpens; (6) Herakles wrestling

Apollon, constellation Gemini; (7) Prometheus and the Caucasian Eagle, constellations Hercules and Aquila; (8) the centaur Cheiron or Pholus, constellation Sagittarius or Centaurus.

105. The constellation now known as Andromeda was thought of as *the stag* by the Sumerian and Akkadians.

106. Shachar, *the morning star*, is found in the mythology of Ugarit as the godling of dawn. As usual, Jesus takes back the rights of the Father to this title—this time through His resurrection claims.

107. These are not perfectly straight lines; they are curved. However, over a fair stretch of continent, they can effectively function as straight.

108. In the episode on the Isle of Deathwater, Lewis links 'taking off armour' with gold, forgetting and bewitchment. In a spiritual sense, this suggests Ziz (Jezebel) is the one who causes us to be careless about the Armour of God. As I've pointed out in *Dealing with Python*, the initial letters of the names of the seven lords—Bern, Octesian, Restimar, Rhoop, Argoz, Revilian, Mavramorn—taken in order spell out 'borrar(u)m', Latin for *of the north wind*. Perhaps they might be therefore considered Boreans or Hyperboreans—a people from beyond the north wind who had allegedly built a magnificent temple to the sungod Apollo.

109. See Jeremiah 8:17.

110. Mephibosheth contains the significant element, 'bosh' or 'besh', *shame*. The name means *end of shame* or *end of dryness*. Yet ironically Mephibosheth wound up in just about the driest place in all of contemporary Israel. Perhaps he went to Lo Debar because it was in the vicinity of Jabesh Gilead, the town whose people had gone out of their way to honour his father and grandfather, risking their lives even in death. Jabesh has the element 'besh' in it, but through honour, the townsfolk had indeed brought an end to shame.

111. The fact that Jesus was driven by the Spirit into the wilderness from Bethany-beyond-the-Jordan suggests He was sent into old Gilead where there were rocks, rocks and more rocks. Perhaps He went to Lo Debar, *the place of no bread*. So that first temptation—to change stones into bread—might have, yet again, been as much about the location as anything else.

112. Archaeological evidence from Wadi El-Yabis, where Jabesh Gilead was located, points to a 'quite significant' level of Phoenician imports. See *Cultural Influences of the Sea Peoples in Transjordan:*

The Early Iron Age at 'Tell Abū Ḥaraz', Peter M. Fischer and Teresa Bürge, *Zeitschrift des Deutschen Palästina-Vereins (1953–)* Bd. 129, H. 2 (2013) Since Beth Shan, on the opposite bank of the Jordan River, was situated on a major trading cross-road both east through the Jezreel Valley to the coast as well as north-south along the Jordan Valley, Gilead wasn't far from a major commercial hub. Although the Midianites of Joseph's day took their own caravan to Egypt, in later times traders came in the opposite direction seeking quality balm.

113. Set was imaged with the head of a jackal, which in Hebrew is 'tan'—the same element as found in Levia*than*.

114. Plutarch became the high priest at the temple of Python Apollo in Delphi during the first century. He wrote on many subjects, including Egyptian religion. In his work on *Isis and Osiris*, he connects the Pythagorean abhorrence of the number 17 with the dismemberment of Osiris.

115. After well over a decade of investigating the extremely favoured position given to the number 17 in early Christian writings, I have reached the conclusion it is used in two senses, one negative and one positive. It is used *against* Pythagorean Gnosticism as the number of 'resurrection' (as opposed to 'reincarnation'), particularly via use of the seventeenth triangular number, 153, the first number that can be resurrected from the sum of the cube of its digits. But a negative reason has never seemed sufficient to me to feature it so prominently and extensively. I've always thought there must be a positive reason, independent of any opposition to a heretical sect. I have come to believe that one positive reason is: 17 is shorthand for 70. In both Greek and Hebrew mathematics, there is often ambiguity about which arithmetic operation to apply: for example, did Jesus advise Peter to forgive his erring brother 70 x 7 or 70 + 7? Actually, it's not clear. So, I've reached the conclusion that 10 + 7 could also point to 10 x 7. Throughout the Torah, seventy represents 'government'—including the division of the nations, as well as the number of elders God invited to dine with Him on Mount Sinai. It's much easier to create multiples of 17 in writing, or lists of 17, rather than of 70. So, for sheer practicality, I believe the early Christian writers used 17 as a code for 70 and that it was, in a positive sense, the symbol for 'spiritual government exercised by the church'. Another positive reason for the use of 17 is that the most archaic form of God's name —I Am—has a numeral value of 17. This archaic form is NOT Yahweh which means *He is who He is*.

116. The legend of Hades involves the abduction of Persephone. Because she ate some pomegranate seeds while in the underworld, she wasn't allowed to return to the normal world permanently but was compelled to spend part of each year as Queen of the Underworld.

117. Even 'distinguished', which is far from being complimentary in some judicial circles. 'My distinguished colleague' euphemistically refers to a judge whose verdicts are out of line with the norm. There are some 'dis' words that are positive, but the overwhelming majority have very negative overtones.

118. The same George MacDonald who wrote *At the Back of the North Wind*.

119. As pointed out in *God's Priority: Generational Testing and World-Mending*, Odin was apparently worshipped about two millennia ago under the name Esus or Hesus. This similarity of this name to Jesus enables Odin to masquerade in some people's lives as a savage, blood-thirsty version of Jesus of Nazareth.

120. The word 'valkyrie' means *the one who chooses those about to be slain*. Odin was aware of a prophecy about the end of time—and that at Ragnarok, the giants would emerge victorious in their war with the godlings and goddesses of Asgard. Nonetheless, he was determined to go down fighting. To that end, he assembled an army by sending out his valkyries to battlefields to escort the most courageous of the slain warriors to his feasting hall at Valhalla. Some of the most famous Norse legends involve valkyries who rebelled against Odin's orders and rescued the hero instead.

121. Numbers 21:4–9 and John 3:14–15

122. The example of Eric Liddell, the champion runner whose story was told in *Chariots of Fire*, would be so unlikely to happen in our century. In 1924, Liddell refused to run in the Olympics heats because they were held on a Sunday and he didn't want to dishonour the Lord's Day. He became an unexpected gold medallist when another runner dropped out of a different event on a weekday and he was given the opportunity to fill in.

123. Most of the Decapolis, *ten towns*, was on the eastern bank of the Jordan river. The ten cities were Gerasa, Gadara, Capitolias, Raphana and Pella in Jordan, Hippos on the Golan Heights, Philadelphia (now Amman, the capital of Jordan), Canatha in Syria, Damascus (now the capital of Syria) and Scythopolis in Israel, the only city west of the Jordan River. In the first century, Scythopolis was the largest of these cities.

124. Scythopolis is believed to mean *City of the Scythians*. According to a legend mentioned by the ancient historians Pliny and Solinus, Dionysus (the Greek god of wine and revelry whom the Romans called Bacchus) founded the city in honour of his nursemaid, Nysa, whom he buried in this spot. He then allegedly settled Scythian archers there to stand watch over her grave. The link between this city as a place once dedicated to an 'archer' deity and then settled by archers seems to indicate the strength of Resheph's spiritual attachment to the location.

125. Henry O. Thompson, *Mekal—The God of Beth Shan*, E.J. Brill, 1970

126. We miss all the clues because, in our culture, the divorce between mathematics and literature was formalised centuries ago and so we focus on fine distinctions in Greek meaning but entirely miss the message of the arithmetic. Sometimes, in my opinion, words were deliberately (not mistakenly) mis-spelled, not because the apostles didn't know better but because they were producing highlighted effects in the gematria. Pythagorean theurgy is a large component of Gnosticism. On the virulent return of Gnosticism in our present age, see, for example, Peter Jones, *The Gnostic Empire Strikes Back: An Old Heresy for a New Age* (Presbyterian and Reformed Publishing Co), which despite being published in 1992 is more relevant than ever.

127. Moreover, for those influenced by Greek thinking, like Hadrian, close enough to an ideal is 'good enough'—even if to the Hebrews, it might have meant 'missing the mark'. In *Dealing with Leviathan*, I suggest this conflict in philosophies is behind the change of the 'Number of the Beast' from 616 to 666.

128. It still retained the name 'Aelia', in the Arabic form 'Iliya', up until the Muslim conquest.

129. According to *The Ancient Paths*, in about 278 B.C., a Celtic warlord by the name of Brennus attacked the sanctuary of Python Apollo in Delphi with the express purposes of relocating it to Gaul. Graham Robb suggests it wasn't the treasure Brennus was after, it was the sanctity of the place itself. He wanted the power of the place to be removed into his own country so the druids there could conveniently and easily access it. The Pythagorean influence in the druidic schools of Gaul and even France during the medieval period is detailed in Christiane L. Joost-Gaugier's *Measuring Heaven: Pythagoras and His Influence on Thought and Art in Antiquity and the Middle Ages*, Cornell University Press 2006

130. It should be pointed out that Leviathan is linked to *trade* in Job 41:6 where the Hebrew word, 'chabbar', is used.

131. behindthename.com/name/resheph/submitted

132. See *Dealing with Ziz: Spirit of Forgetting: Strategies for the Threshold #2*, Armour Books, 2018.

133. *Stag* can also be, depending on context, *oak*, *ram*, *pillar*, *mighty man* or even, at not too great a stretch, *morning star*. In places where the context is uncertain (such as Psalm 29:9), the translations reflect this. Since the primary meaning is simply *strong leader*, in terms of the resurrection, Jesus was a *strong leader*: as our Captain, He was the firstborn from the dead.

134. In Hittite, Reshef is identified with a protection god, and is also very often called Teshup, Hadad or Baal. The other word that may be connected with the name Reshef is Arsippus, the father of (the third) Asclepius, mentioned by Cicero. This Arsippus together with Arsinoe, both having an Egyptian origin, are mentioned as the parents of Asclepius. According to Plutarch, Ariston, in his book *Colonies of the Athenians* states that Dionysus in Egypt was called not Osiris, but Arsaphes. See: Krzysztof Ulanowski, *God Reshef in the Mediterranean*, in: SOMA 2012. *Identity and Connectivity: Proceedings of the 16th Symposium on Mediterranean Archaeology*, Florence, Italy, 1–3 March 2012, vol. 1, (ed.) L. Bombardieri, A. D'Agostino, V. Orsi, Archaeopress, Oxford 2013

135. Mammon and Melqart are the same and, like them, the mythical Asian beast, the qilin, claims guardianship of money. Special worship of the qilin occurs once every sixty or seventy years in China. This one-horned beast is said to look terrifying but to be so gentle and peaceful it walks on clouds to avoid harming the grass. Like Leviathan, the qilin has dragon attributes and impenetrable scales and is also connected with a whale. Like Resheph, it is envisaged, on the one hand as horse or unicorn-like, and on the other as having the antlers of a deer and being in charge of health and longevity. Like Baal Hadad, it is a cloud-rider or more accurately, 'cloud-stepper'.

'Chinese ancestor worship is a foundational aspect of Chinese traditional folk religion. Deified ancestors, and their ghosts or spirits, are considered part of this world. A person is thought to have multiple souls, categorised as *hun* and *po*. Upon death, *hun* and *po* separate with the former ascending into heaven while *po* remains on earth, residing within a spirit tablet. Chinese funerary customs involve setting up [an] altar for prayer, sometimes decorating with white flowers, the colour associated with death and mourning in China. Incense and oil lamps burn for the full time of mourning, while the children of the family sleep on the floor to ward off evil spirits. For seven days after the funeral, the deceased person's favourite food alongside joss paper and 'Hell Money' is placed on the altar and burnt to provide the deceased with their favourite possessions in the next world. If the family is wealthy, they may also burn paper houses, boats and clothing. Many Chinese people observe the Qingming or Ching Ming, an annual day when families visit and clean the graves of their ancestors, pray and make ritual offerings.' (Bendigo Museum)

In cultures across the world, symbols of these underworld deities morph in a way that suits the society while their origin still remains recognisable. Janine, a Cook Islander, considers that the Maori story of the whale-rider—which originates on the tiny Pacific island of Mauke where some of Janine's ancestors come from—is a transparent shift in spiritual understanding away from Jesus the cloud-rider.

136. Resheph is considered by some adherents of Jainism to be 'Rishabha'; Arsuf is Arabic for Resheph.

137. As I've indicated in the analysis in *Dealing with Ziz: Spirit of Forgetting*, both her names as well as the decree Jesus spoke over her life at Bethany indicate this is so.

138. A bit like Saint Sebastian, who perhaps not surprisingly is the patron saint of plague. Arrows and plague retained a long association throughout millennia. Sebastian's name comes from Sebaste, formerly Samaria. When Caesar Augustus gave this ancient town to Herod the Great in 30 BC, Herod renamed it Sebaste, *great*, the Greek feminine form of the Roman name Augustus.

139. In Ephesians 6:16, Paul exhorts us to hold up the shield of faith to extinguish the flaming arrows of the Evil One—a description that suggests the 'Evil One' in question is Resheph.

Dealing with Rachab:
Spirit of Wasting

Strategies for the Threshold #11

The spirit of wasting is not hard to overcome if you've first mastered the spirit of rejection. However, she's not going to take defeat quietly, so she marshals the other threshold guardians in a combined assault. Their primary agenda is to ensure we're tied up in an unbreakable double bind.

As we examine Scripture, we'll note that the double binds mentioned there always involve denial of access to the atonement. We can't lose our salvation, but we can lose some of its temporal benefits. Even Jesus didn't find dismantling such double binds easy, but He provides us with a way forward.

www.ingramcontent.com/pod-product-compliance
Lightning Source LLC
Chambersburg PA
CBHW021833110526
R18278200001B/R182782PG44588CBX00010B/15